THE
CHRISTMAS MOVIE
COOKBOOK

THE CHRISTMAS MOVIE COOKBOOK

RECIPES FROM YOUR FAVORITE HOLIDAY FILMS

JULIA RUTLAND

SIMON ELEMENT

NEW YORK   LONDON   TORONTO   SYDNEY   NEW DELHI

SIMON
ELEMENT

An Imprint of Simon & Schuster, Inc.
1230 Avenue of the Americas
New York, NY 10020

First Simon Element hardcover edition September 2022

SIMON ELEMENT is a trademark of Simon & Schuster, Inc.

For information about special discounts for bulk purchases, please contact
Simon & Schuster Special Sales at 1-866-506-1949 or business@simonandschuster.com.

The Simon & Schuster Speakers Bureau can bring authors to your live event. For more
information or to book an event, contact the Simon & Schuster Speakers Bureau at
1-866-248-3049 or visit our website at www.simonspeakers.com.

Interior design by Matt Ryan
Photography produced by Blueline Creative Group LLC.
Visit: www.bluelinecreativegroup.com
Producer: Katherine Cobbs
Photographer: Caitlin Bensel
Food Stylist: McLean
Food Stylist Assistant: S. McKay, Gordon Sawyer
Prop Stylist: Kay Clarke

Manufactured in China

10 9 8 7 6 5 4 3 2 1

Library of Congress Cataloging-in-Publication Data
Names: Rutland, Julia Dowling, author.
Title: The Christmas movie cookbook : over 65 recipes of cinematic holiday delights / by Julia Rutland.
Description: New York : Simon Element, 2022. | Includes index.
Identifiers: LCCN 2021053272 (print) | LCCN 2021053273 (ebook) | ISBN 9781982189372
(hardcover) | ISBN 9781982189389 (ebook)
Subjects: LCSH: Christmas cooking. | Seasonal cooking. | Christmas films.
Classification: LCC TX739.2.C45 .R88 2022 (print) | LCC TX739.2.C45 (ebook) |
DDC 641.5/686—dc23/eng/20211216
LC record available at https://lccn.loc.gov/2021053272
LC ebook record available at https://lccn.loc.gov/2021053273

ISBN 978-1-9821-8937-2
ISBN 978-1-9821-8938-9 (ebook)

CONTENTS

INTRODUCTION

When I was growing up, cartoons were only shown on weekends, and Christmas specials aired once on a single evening sometime after Thanksgiving, making the viewings even more special. The first holiday feature I remember watching on TV is *A Charlie Brown Christmas*. Each year I would be giddy with anticipation for that special night when it would air. It would be a big deal to rush through dinner and carve out a bit of space on the sofa, patiently waiting for whatever program aired beforehand to be over. While I don't remember each viewing, I do remember the absolute heartache I felt one year when I fell asleep on the comfy pillows and didn't wake up until the Peanuts gang sang, "Hark! The Herald Angels Sing." I was inconsolable. At the time, I thought I was grieving a missed cartoon; however, adult me realizes that my younger self lost a special holiday tradition I unknowingly created and celebrated with the passion of any believing seven-year-old.

Nowadays any programming can be downloaded, rented, or purchased for quick viewing any day of the year. But the idea of watching holiday movies is still a treasured tradition. Whether you binge-watch a variety of shows, power through a single movie marathon, or simply catch a random program while you wrap presents, Christmas movies create important memories.

The movies that inspired the recipes in this book run the gamut. Their tones range from innocent and spiritual to irreverent and downright bawdy. There are movies that were released in the early 1940s in black and white, while some premiered via streaming services in the 2020s. There are animated shorts, classic Hollywood musicals, heartwarming romantic comedies, and action flicks. I wanted the movies and their accompanying recipes in this book to be as inclusive as possible—I'm willing to bet that there is something for every holiday movie lover and every palate. Cocktails are paired with adult-only films, while movies aimed at the younger set have kid-type foods that everyone will enjoy. There'll be a little crossover—the salted caramel milkshake appeals to all ages, but I don't encourage a family viewing of the movie pairing (*Anna and the Apocalypse*). Parents should use their best judgment, so take a look at the online reviews to see if a film is a good fit for your family (but still try the recipe!).

Some movies may not be "Christmas-y enough" for some viewers, but much of the fun lies in the eternal debate over what defines a Christmas movie. Likewise, some of the recipes are not strictly "holiday" and can be made any day of the year, but they appear in or relate to the plot of a film. I tried to find a recipe to obviously match each movie, but sometimes the movie didn't lend itself to an easy pairing. In that case, I developed a typical holiday recipe that is common or iconic to the country where the movie is set or somehow associated with one of the main characters.

Take, for example, the delightfully written and superbly animated film *Klaus*, a movie aimed at older children but with enough double entendres to entertain adults. Yes, the film is definitely Christmas-themed—the plot involves sending letters to Santa—but there are no food scenes. One of the characters used to be a schoolteacher, but with no kids in her class, she resorts to becoming a fishmonger. So, what kind of seafood recipe would appeal to kids? Potato chip–crusted fish sticks of course!

I fully believe that life is about the journey and not the destination. The same applies to planning for the holidays. There's excitement in all the processes of getting ready, from decorating, buying gifts, marathon baking, and planning the menus. For die-hard Christmas fans, these tasks are comforting rituals. Anyone who gets a sense of melancholy when the last wreath and holiday ornament are tucked into their boxes, leaving the house a bit bare, knows exactly what I mean. So it's been a joy to extend the holiday season into the summer in order to produce this book, and I couldn't have done it alone.

Much gratitude goes out to Ronnie Alvarado for shepherding me thought the development and writing process; Katherine Cobb, Caitlin Bensel, and Kay Clarke for creating the lovely images; Matt Ryan for the interior design; and the rest of the helpful staff at Simon Element for getting this book out into the world.

Thanks to everyone who helped me taste-test these recipes and give me feedback: Vicki and John, Sharon and Brian, Paige and Larry, Karen, Kristen, Rhonda, Eric and Katie, Jeff and Cynthia, Ingrid and Joe, Danielle and Dennis, Nick, Randi, Jackie, Susan, and the crew at Noble Athletics, who unknowingly tasted at potluck picnics.

Much love and my biggest thanks goes out to my ever-supportive husband, Dit, and daughters, E. Bishop and Corinne—they really enjoyed this book, because there were so many movies and sweet treats!

Entertaining Tips

There are few events more special than holiday gatherings with friends and loved ones. And why not add a little extra Christmas cheer by watching your favorite holiday movie during the party? As you plan, keep in mind some of these pro tips to make sure that the occasion stays merry and bright.

VIEWING PARTIES SHOULD GENERALLY BE KEPT ON THE SMALLER SIDE since everyone needs a comfortable place to sit and a clear view of the screen. Make sure every seat has a surface close by to hold drinks and plates.

IF WATCHING A MOVIE ACCESSED ONLINE, download early, if possible, to avoid any buffering snafus.

NOT IN THE MOOD TO HOST PEOPLE OR SHELTERING IN PLACE? Plan a remote watch party. Various subscription services offer these shared viewing options if all the participants are members.

REARRANGE YOUR LIVING SPACE to create conversation nooks for pre- and post-viewing, and paths for guests to meander to and from food and drink.

CONSIDER THE THEME OF THE MOVIE and ask guests to dress in similar costumes to that aesthetic. Or have guests dress like characters in their own favorite holiday movie!

HAVE A PLAYLIST READY with enough songs to keep repeats to a minimum. Make sure the volume is low enough for easy conversation.

SET THE MOOD WITH DÉCOR! You don't need expensive matching tableware or elaborate floral arrangements—unless you love it, in which case, go for it! An easy idea is to drape some garland in the center of the table and top with pine cones and a few small round ornaments. Level up with some battery-operated mini white lights hidden within any greenery.

A FULL BAR REQUIRES a variety of spirits and even more mixers. A low-stress and budget-friendly way to offer adult beverages to a group is to serve one specialty cocktail, rounded out with basic beer and wine.

THE AMOUNT OF LIQUOR TO HAVE available depends on the guests and how long the party will last. At minimum, plan on two drinks per adult guest.

PLAN THE MENU well in advance so there's time to prepare make-ahead dishes.

SERVE FOODS IN A VARIETY OF COLORS AND TEXTURES— a wide array of fruits and vegetables is often healthier than a lot of beige starches.

CHOOSE RECIPES REQUIRING DIFFERENT COOKING TECHNIQUES so you don't overload your oven or cooktop.

CONSIDER A WIDE RANGE OF DIETS and have both gluten-free or low-fat options available. Or serve toppings on the side so guests can accommodate their needs. Additionally, ask guests if they have any food allergies like nuts or shellfish.

IF SERVING COCKTAILS, while waiting for all the guests arrive, offer finger foods like spiced nuts, crudité, or crackers and cheese for those particularly hungry attendees to nibble on.

FOR COCKTAIL OR BUFFET PARTIES, serve individual portions or pre-sliced foods to avoid bottlenecks at the table as others wait for each piece to be cut. Preportion foods into bites small enough to avoid needing a knife. Bite-size food will also be easier to eat on laps if guests are sitting.

IF SKIPPING FLATWARE, make sure all foods can be picked up with fingers without a mess. Utilize wooden picks or small skewers.

KEEP TABLECLOTH SPILLS TO A MINIMUM and place sauce and gravy bowls on larger plates to collect the inevitable drips down the side. If any salad dressings separate, place them in a container with a lid for shaking before drizzling, or in a bowl so they can be stirred with a small ladle.

Holiday Menu Ideas

Round out your Christmas movie viewing party feast or create a variety of holiday meals with these menu suggestions—see if your guests can mix and match the food with the movies!

HOLIDAY OPEN HOUSE DESSERT PARTY

Really Rich Hot Chocolate (page 13)
Eggnog (page 14)
Spiced Pumpkin Tarts (page 138)
Red Velvet Cupcakes (page 144)
Sugar Plums (page 126)
Naughty or Nice Gingerbread Men (page 118)
Chocolate-Pecan Snowballs (page 122)
Three-Layer Mint Brownies (page 130)

HOLIDAY BUFFET FOR A CROWD

Spiked Spiced Cider (page 19)
Really Rich Hot Chocolate (page 13)
Hickory-Honey Ham (page 108)
Creamy Mashed Potatoes (page 68)
Spiced Pumpkin Tarts (page 138)
Three-Layer Mint Brownies (page 130)
Sugar Cookies with Lots of Sprinkles (page 114)

HOLIDAY BREAK SLEEPOVER

Plain Cheese Pizza (page 73)
Salted Caramel & Fudge Milkshake (page 16)
Giant Chocolate Chunk Cookies (page 117)

VINTAGE SUNDAY DINNER IN DECEMBER

Old-Fashioned Meatloaf (page 97)
Creamy Mashed Potatoes (page 68)
Mixed green salad
"Peanuts" Butter Cookies (page 121)

DECK-THE-HALLS TREE DECORATING PARTY

Mocha Martini (page 29)
Spiked Spiced Cider (page 19)
Chicken Potpie (page 88)
Quinoa, Kale & Sweet Potato Salad (page 63)
    Or simple mixed green salad
Chocolate-Pecan Snowballs (page 122)

HOLIDAY DINNER

Quinoa, Kale & Sweet Potato Salad (page 63)
Hickory-Honey Ham (page 108)
Creamy Mashed Potatoes (page 68)
Roasted Brussels sprouts
Japanese Christmas Cake (page 151)

FEAST OF ST. NICHOLAS

Rosemary Bee's Knees (page 24)
(Quicker) Chicken, Sausage & White Bean
    Cassoulet (page 83)
Chapati (page 39) or warm French bread
Mixed green salad
Bûche de Noël (page 153)

SIMPLIFIED FEAST OF SEVEN FISHES

Brown Sugar–Cured Salmon with Zesty Mustard
    Sauce (page 51)
Insalata di Mare (Italian Seafood Salad) (page 65)
Crispy Fish Sticks (page 76)
Marinara Sauce for Spaghetti (page 98)
White Chocolate–Espresso Shortbread (page 123)

ASSEMBLING-TOYS-BEFORE-DAWN SNACKS

Whiskey-Pomegranate Sour (page 20)
Grilled Ham & Cheese on Rye (page 74)
Giant Chocolate Chunk Cookies (page 117)

CHRISTMAS BRUNCH FOR A CROWD

Coffee
Cranberry Sparklers (page 23)
Brown Sugar–Cured Salmon with Zesty Mustard Sauce (page 51)
Breakfast Strata (page 33)
Hickory-Honey Ham (page 108)
Overnight Orange-Cinnamon Rolls (page 37)
Three-Layer Eggnog Cake (page 148)

GRAND ENGLISH FEAST

Eggnog (page 14)
Christmas Mule (page 27)
Garlic-&-Herb-Crusted Roast Beef (page 101)
Horseradish Cream Sauce (page 102)
Creamy Mashed Potatoes (page 68)
Glazed carrots and parsnips
Creamed spinach
Yorkshire Pudding with Herbs (page 43)
Christmas Pudding (page 140)

TRADITIONAL CHRISTMAS DINNER

Spiked Spiced Cider (page 19)
Roast Goose with Onion & Sage Gravy (page 92)
    Or Roast Turkey with Pomegranate Sauce (page 90)
Stuffing or dressing
Creamy Mashed Potatoes (page 68)
Green Beans or green bean casserole
Cranberry sauce
Sweet Potato Pie (page 129)

NEW YEAR'S EVE NOSH

Cranberry Sparklers (page 23)
Eggnog (page 14)
Brown Sugar–Cured Salmon with Zesty Mustard Sauce (page 51)
Pigs in a Blanket (page 47)
Guacamole-Stuffed Eggs (page 48)
Linzer Star Cookies (page 125)
White Chocolate–Espresso Shortbread (page 123)

KEEP-WARM-CAROLING AFTER PARTY

Really Rich Hot Chocolate (page 13)
Spiked Spiced Cider (page 19)
Chicken, Broccoli & Cheddar Soup (page 54)
Warm sliced artisan bread
Naughty or Nice Gingerbread Men (page 118)

HOLIDAY BOWL GAME NOSH

Whiskey-Pomegranate Sour (page 20)
Seafood & Sausage Gumbo (page 53)
Baby Back Ribs (page 109)
Baked Buffalo Wings (page 78)
Sugar Cookies with Lots of Sprinkles (page 114)
Caramel Corn (page 128)

LIGHT AND HEALTHY NEW YEAR'S DINNER

Egg Drop Soup (page 59)
Quinoa, Kale & Sweet Potato Salad (page 63)
Rotisserie Chicken (page 87)
Angel Food Cake (page 147)

BEVERAGES

REALLY RICH
HOT CHOCOLATE

⟶ MAKES 6 CUPS ⟵

If you have a crowd to serve, you can double or triple the recipe, depending on how many servings you need. It's easy if you make this richly decadent hot chocolate in a slow cooker using low heat. The mild heat melts the chocolate and sugars and only requires occasional stirring.

4 cups whole milk

2 cups half-and-half

½ cup granulated sugar

¼ cup firmly packed light brown sugar

8-ounce bar semisweet or dark chocolate, chopped

½ cup unsweetened cocoa powder

1 tablespoon vanilla extract

Mini marshmallows, for serving

Whipped cream, for serving

1. In a heavy saucepan, combine the milk, half-and-half, sugars, chocolate, cocoa powder, and vanilla. Cook over low heat, whisking frequently, until the chocolate melts and the mixture is smooth.

2. Ladle into cups and serve with marshmallows and/or whipped cream.

POLAR EXPRESS
(2004)

All aboard! In this animated interpretation of Chris Van Allsburg's 1985 book of the same name, a young boy travels to the North Pole aboard a classic steam train, the Polar Express, thus renewing his belief in Santa Claus. With Tom Hanks voicing the majority of the adult characters, the film is a delightful foray into the magic of Christmas. In a particularly toe-tapping scene, a chorus of singing and dancing waiters delivers hot chocolate to the young boy and his fellow travelers, starting their journey off with a tasty treat.

THE FAMILY MAN
(2000)

What would your life have been like if you had chosen a different path? In this holiday romantic comedy starring Nicholas Cage, Don Cheadle, and Téa Leoni, high-powered businessman Jack Campbell gets a taste of the "what if" while en route to buy some holiday eggnog. Save yourself the trip to the convenience store and brew your own holiday treat instead.

EGGNOG

⇀ MAKES 8 CUPS (WITH BEATEN EGG WHITES) ↽

While there are many variations of this silky holiday drink, the base of any eggnog is a mix of milk or cream, sugar, and eggs. You can make the recipe without the rum and simply add a shot of liquor in the bottom of each glass for those guests who want a spiked version. Adding beaten egg whites just before serving is optional, but it creates a lighter texture.

⅔ cup granulated sugar

¾ teaspoon ground nutmeg

8 large eggs

2 cups heavy whipping cream

2 cups whole milk

1 teaspoon vanilla extract

¾ cup rum, cognac, or bourbon (optional)

Cinnamon stick, ground cinnamon, and/or ground nutmeg, for garnish (optional)

1. In a bowl, stir together the sugar and nutmeg. Separate the eggs and add the yolks to the sugar mixture, whisking well. Cover and refrigerate the egg whites until ready to use in this recipe or for other uses, such as an egg-white omelet.

2. In a medium saucepan, combine the cream and milk. Cook over medium heat, stirring frequently, just until the mixture begins to simmer (do not boil).

3. Whisk ¼ cup of the hot cream mixture into the egg mixture. Repeat twice more with another ¼ cup of the cream mixture. Pour the combined mixture into the hot cream mixture.

4. Cook, stirring constantly, until the mixture reaches 160°F on a thermometer (this may happen quickly, depending on how warm the cream mixture is). Remove from the heat and stir in the vanilla and liquor, if desired.

5. Cover and chill for several hours or up to a day ahead. The mixture will thicken as it cools. If desired and just before serving, beat the egg whites with an electric mixer until soft peaks form and fold them into the chilled eggnog. Serve with a cinnamon stick or a pinch of ground cinnamon or ground nutmeg, if desired.

ANNA AND THE APOCALYPSE

(2017)

A Christmas-themed zombie movie musical, this unexpected and little-known British romp gives a whole new meaning to "it's beginning to look a lot like Christmas."

SALTED CARAMEL & FUDGE MILKSHAKE

→ SERVES 2 TO 4 ←

Homemade ice cream takes this shake to the next level. If time prohibits making your own, use the best grocery store ice cream you can find. While commercial ice cream can handle a lengthy storage time in the freezer, homemade ice cream loses flavor more rapidly, so make this recipe only up to two weeks in advance. (It's so tasty that it won't last that long anyway!)

1½ cups whole milk

2 pints (4 cups) Salted Caramel Ice Cream (recipe follows)

⅓ cup dark chocolate sauce or chocolate syrup, plus more for serving

Whipped cream, for serving (optional)

Sprinkles, for garnish (optional)

1. In a blender, combine the milk and ice cream. Pulse several times until well blended.

2. Drizzle the inside walls of two glasses evenly with the fudge sauce and pour in the milkshake. Top with whipped cream, additional sauce, and/or sprinkles, if desired.

SALTED CARAMEL ICE CREAM

⇢ MAKES 1½ QUARTS ⇠

2 cups heavy whipping cream

2 cups whole milk

8 large egg yolks

1 cup granulated sugar

¼ cup water

1 teaspoon vanilla extract

½ teaspoon flaky sea salt

1. Combine the cream and milk in a medium saucepan. Cook over medium heat, stirring occasionally, until warm (do not boil). Cover and keep warm.

2. In a small bowl, whisk the egg yolks.

3. Combine the sugar and water in a heavy saucepan over medium heat. Cook for 2 minutes, stirring occasionally, until the sugar melts. Stop stirring and cook for 5 to 7 minutes, swirling the pan occasionally, until the sugar mixture turns a dark caramel brown.

4. Remove from the heat and slowly pour the cream mixture into the caramel (mixture will boil vigorously). The caramel may harden on the bottom of the pan. Reheat, stirring frequently, over medium-low heat until the caramel melts and the mixture is completely blended.

5. Slowly drizzle about 1 cup of the caramel mixture into the egg yolks, whisking constantly. Repeat twice. Whisk the egg mixture into the remaining caramel mixture to create a custard.

6. Cook the custard mixture over medium-low heat, stirring frequently, until the mixture thickens slightly and registers 170°F on a thermometer (do not allow to boil). If necessary, pour the custard through a fine mesh strainer to remove any lumps. Cool to room temperature and stir in the vanilla and sea salt. Cover and chill for several hours or overnight until completely cold.

7. Process the custard mixture in a 2-quart or larger ice cream maker according to the manufacturer's instructions. Serve immediately for soft ice cream or cover and freeze until firm.

Spiked Spiced Cider

→ MAKES 8 CUPS ←

Although they are both made from apples, fresh cider differs from juice or shelf-stable cider in that it has not been filtered and contains pulp and solids. Fresh cider isn't pasteurized and may ferment if not refrigerated.

½ gallon (64 ounces) fresh apple cider

1 orange, thickly sliced

5 cinnamon sticks, plus more for garnish

1 (1-inch) piece fresh ginger root, peeled and sliced

2 teaspoons whole cloves

2 teaspoons whole allspice

4 star anise pods (optional)

1½ cups spiced rum

Orange slices, for garnish (optional)

In a Dutch oven or soup pot, combine the cider, orange slices, cinnamon, ginger, cloves, allspice, and star anise, if using. Cook over medium-low heat for 1 hour. Remove the spices with a slotted spoon. Stir in the rum. Garnish with orange slices and/or cinnamon sticks, if desired.

A BAD MOMS CHRISTMAS
(2017)

Raunchy, irreverent, and a whole lot of fun, this sequel to the 2016 comedy *Bad Moms* features best friends Amy (Mila Kunis), Kiki (Kristen Bell), and Carla (Kathryn Hahn) attempting to regain control of Christmas after their own moms drop in unexpectedly for the holidays. While at their wits' end on a trip to a local mall, the trio elevates basic cider to an outrageous level by adding more than a dash of spiced rum, and mayhem ensues. You can make this version of spiced cider family-friendly by skipping the rum.

(2003)

Billy Bob Thornton stars as plotting conman Willie in this dark comedy that gives a whole new meaning to the phrase "Christmas spirit." Featuring unforgettable performances from Lauren Graham, Brett Kelly, Tony Cox, Bernie Mac, and John Ritter, the film is perfect for an adults-only holiday watch party. While Willie has no problem downing straight, inexpensive booze, we recommend this delightful mixed drink to create holiday cheer.

WHISKEY-POMEGRANATE SOUR

⇢ SERVES 1 ⇠

To give holiday flair to a basic whiskey-amaretto sour, add a bit of pomegranate juice. Its bitterness offsets the sweetness of the amaretto, giving the cocktail complex flavor and a cheerful color.

1½ ounces (3 tablespoons) whiskey or bourbon

1½ ounces (3 tablespoons) amaretto liqueur

2 tablespoons pomegranate juice

1 tablespoon Sour Mix (recipe follows)

Dash bitters

Lemon and/or lime slices, for garnish (optional)

Pomegranate arils, for garnish (optional)

Combine the whiskey, liqueur, juice, Sour Mix, and bitters in an ice-filled cocktail shaker. Shake vigorously and pour into an ice-filled glass. Garnish with lemon and lime slices and/or pomegranate arils, if desired.

SOUR MIX

⇢ MAKES ¾ CUP ⇠

¼ cup granulated sugar

¼ cup hot water

¼ cup fresh lemon juice

2 tablespoons fresh lime juice

In a small saucepan, combine the sugar and water. Cook over low heat, stirring until sugar melts. Let stand until cool. Stir in the lemon and lime juices. Cover and refrigerate for two weeks or until ready to use.

CRANBERRY SPARKLERS

✢ SERVES 8 ✢

Candied orange peel is best homemade but can be ordered online for convenience. If you have extra, substitute it for raisins or dried cranberries in recipes, or dip half of it in melted dark chocolate for a small but decadent treat.

1 cup unsweetened cranberry juice plus more for serving, chilled

¼ cup sparkling, turbanado, or granulated sugar

4 ounces (½ cup) orange liqueur, chilled

1 (750-milliliter) bottle sparkling wine, chilled

Candied orange peel, for garnish (optional)

Fresh or frozen cranberries, for garnish (optional)

1. Dip the rim of 8 champagne flutes in the cranberry juice, allowing the excess to drip off. Then dip the rims into the sugar.

2. Pour 2 tablespoons of the cranberry juice and ½ ounce (1 tablespoon) of the orange liqueur into each of the glasses. Top with the sparkling wine. Garnish with candied orange peels and cranberries, if desired.

THE BEST MAN HOLIDAY
(2013)

Break out the tissues for this funny and heartwarming sequel to the 1999 dramedy *The Best Man*. The original ensemble cast—Taye Diggs, Sanaa Lathan, Nia Long, Morris Chestnut, Harold Perrineau, Terrence Howard, Monica Calhoun, Melissa De Sousa, and Regina Hall—returns to celebrate Christmas together. This sparkling aperitif will get you in an equally festive mood as you gather together and toast long-lasting friendships.

A dramedy all about honesty, love, and acceptance, *Happiest Season* is a heartwarming modern classic perfect for a watch party with older kids. The all-star cast features Kristen Stewart and Mackenzie Davis in leading roles, with charming and hysterical performances by Dan Levy, Alison Brie, Aubrey Plaza, Mary Holland, Mary Steenburgen, and Victor Garber.

ROSEMARY BEE'S KNEES

⇢ SERVES 1 ⇠

A typical Bee's Knees cocktail consists of gin, fresh lemon, and honey syrup. This version infuses aromatic rosemary in the honey syrup, giving the drink a complex flavor. Serve shaken and strained into a coupe glass or, for an even lighter version, pour over ice in a rocks glass and top with club soda.

2 ounces (¼ cup) gin

¾ ounce (1½ tablespoons) fresh lemon juice

¾ ounce (1½ tablespoons) Rosemary-Honey Syrup (recipe follows)

Fresh lemon twist, for garnish (optional)

Fresh rosemary sprig, for garnish (optional)

Combine the gin, lemon juice, and Rosemary-Honey Syrup in an ice-filled cocktail shaker. Shake vigorously and strain into a coupe glass. Garnish with the lemon and rosemary, if desired.

ROSEMARY-HONEY SYRUP

Use a mild honey such as alfalfa, clover, or orange blossom so it doesn't overpower the rosemary.

½ cup honey

½ cup water

3 (5-inch) fresh rosemary sprigs

In a medium saucepan over medium-high heat, combine the honey, water, and rosemary. Bring to a boil, reduce heat to low, and simmer for 5 minutes or until the honey dissolves. While the mixture cooks, press the rosemary sprigs against the bottom and sides of the pan to muddle. Remove the rosemary-honey mixture from the heat and let stand for 1 hour or until completely cooled. Strain to remove the rosemary. Store in the refrigerator up to two weeks.

CHRISTMAS MULE

⊱ SERVES 1 ⊰

A popular cocktail developed in the 1940s, a standard Moscow Mule features vodka and ginger beer. This version adds a bit of blood orange liqueur, which imparts an exotic flavor. Ginger is a classic holiday spice, so this recipe doubles down with a sliver of crystallized ginger as a garnish.

1 ounce (2 tablespoons) blood orange liqueur

1 ounce (2 tablespoons) vodka

¾ ounce (1½ tablespoons) fresh lime juice

Dash orange or other bitters

½ cup ginger beer

Candied ginger slices, for garnish (optional)

Blood orange twists or slices, for garnish (optional)

Combine the liqueur, vodka, lime juice, and bitters in an ice-filled copper mug, rocks glass, or Collins glass. Stir in the ginger beer. Garnish with candied ginger and orange twists or slices, if desired.

REMEMBER THE NIGHT
(1940)

While this classic black-and-white film has a few equally comedic and melancholy moments, at its core, *Remember the Night* is a heartwarming romance. Starring Fred MacMurray and Barbara Stanwyck as an attorney and a thief, respectively, whose opposites-attract relationship deepens when each character is willing to change their ways for the other. Tender and sincere, it's sure to fill you with the joy of the season.

MOCHA MARTINI

⟶ SERVES 1 ⟵

Hard-shell chocolate coating stays put on a glass, but liquid chocolate sauce works, too, if the glass is chilled first. The brewed coffee shouldn't be warm, so if you are making it just before serving, brew it very strong and add a few ice cubes to chill quickly.

Hard-shell chocolate or dark chocolate sauce

2 ounces (4 tablespoons) coffee liqueur

1½ ounces (3 tablespoons) brewed coffee, cold or room temperature

1½ ounces (3 tablespoons) Créme de Cacao liqueur

Chocolate-filled rolled wafer cookies or chocolate-dipped biscuit stick cookies, for garnish (optional)

1. Place martini glasses in the freezer for 5 minutes to chill. Dip or roll the rims in the chocolate sauce.

2. Combine the coffee liqueur, coffee, and Créme de Cacao in an ice-filled cocktail shaker. Shake vigorously and pour into a martini or other glass. Garnish with the cookies, if desired.

A CHRISTMAS MOVIE CHRISTMAS

(2019)

Sisters Eve and Lacy have vastly different views on Christmas—one's a romantic, while the other is a bit jaded. After they each make secret wishes, the pair wake up to a world where they live out every holiday romance trope and get their happily-ever-after Christmas. While the over-the-top clichés might make you wince, the film delightfully introduces the term "Scrinch"—a combination of Scrooge and Grinch. It's the perfect holiday flick for a drinking game with all the nods to holiday stereotypes, but a fair warning: the film is packed with them, so proceed with caution. As an alternative, just sip on this tempting cocktail with your besties.

BREAKFAST & BREADS

LITTLE WOMEN
(1933, 1949, 1994, AND 2019)

No matter which of the film adaptions of Louisa May Alcott's classic novel *Little Women* you watch, Christmas morning at Orchard House with the Marches is a joyous and festive occasion. In a story filled with touching moments, one of the most poignant occurs early on when Marmee encourages her daughters Jo, Meg, Beth, and Amy to give up their Christmas breakfast to an impoverished family nearby. Among the delights served at the Marches' Christmas morning feast are housekeeper Hannah's buckwheat pancakes. Hearty and flavorful, these pancakes will fill your body and spirit with warmth and comfort.

BUCKWHEAT PANCAKES

→ MAKES 12 PANCAKES ←

Buckwheat isn't a form of wheat or a grain; rather it is a seed related to rhubarb. It is naturally gluten-free and has a low glycemic index. Used at 100 percent, it can be dense, so it is often mixed with conventional flour. This recipe allows for gluten-free baking mixes instead of flour, if desired.

1 cup buckwheat flour

1 cup all-purpose flour

2 tablespoons granulated sugar

1 teaspoon baking powder

½ teaspoon baking soda

½ teaspoon fine sea salt

¼ teaspoon ground cinnamon

2 large eggs

2 cups buttermilk

4 tablespoons unsalted butter, melted

1 tablespoon oil or melted butter

Maple syrup, for serving

Peeled and sliced oranges and/or blueberries, for serving (optional)

1. Preheat the oven to 200°F.

2. In a medium bowl, combine the flours, sugar, baking powder, baking soda, salt, and cinnamon. In a separate large bowl, whisk the eggs. Stir in the buttermilk and melted unsalted butter. Add the dry ingredients to the wet ingredients, stirring just until combined. Do not overmix.

3. Heat a nonstick griddle or skillet over medium heat. Brush very lightly with about ½ teaspoon of the oil. For each pancake, ladle ⅓ cup batter onto the hot surface. Cook for 2 to 3 minutes or until the bottom is golden brown and bubbles form on the top. Flip over and cook for 1 to 2 minutes or until cooked thoroughly. Cook in batches, repeating with remaining oil and batter.

4. Place the cooked pancakes in the oven to keep warm while remaining pancakes cook. Serve with the maple syrup and top with oranges and blueberries, if desired.

ℬREAKFAST 𝔖TRATA

→ SERVES 8 ←

Stratas make excellent morning meals since they are prepared the night before, allowing the bread to soak up the eggy custard before it's baked to a beautiful golden brown color. If you want to add meat, stir in a cup of chopped ham or six slices of cooked and crumbled bacon with the arugula. If your bread is fresh, place out on a counter, uncovered, until it is dry and somewhat firm.

3 tablespoons salted butter, plus more for the baking dish	1 cup (4 ounces) shredded Gouda cheese, divided
1 large onion, chopped	12 large eggs
2 garlic cloves, minced	3 cups whole milk or half-and-half
1 (5-ounce) container baby arugula	1½ teaspoons fine sea salt
2 roasted red bell peppers, drained and chopped	1 teaspoon dried oregano
16 ounces stale sourdough or another artisan bread, cubed	½ teaspoon ground black pepper
1 cup (4 ounces) shredded sharp cheddar cheese, divided	

1. Butter a 13x9-inch or 3-quart baking dish.

2. In a large skillet, melt the butter over medium heat. Add the onion. Cook, stirring frequently, for 7 to 10 minutes or until tender and beginning to turn golden brown. Add the garlic. Cook, stirring frequently, for 1 minute. Stir in the arugula. Cover and cook for 5 minutes or until wilted and tender. Stir in the roasted bell peppers.

3. Arrange the bread evenly over the bottom of the prepared baking dish. Add half of the cheddar and Gouda, tossing to combine. Add the onion mixture, tossing gently to lightly combine.

4. In a large bowl, combine the eggs, milk, salt, oregano, and pepper, whisking until well blended. Pour the egg mixture over the bread mixture, pressing the bread down to soak completely. Cover with foil and refrigerate for 8 hours or overnight.

5. Preheat the oven to 350°F. Bake the strata, covered, for 40 minutes. Uncover and sprinkle with the remaining cheese. Bake for 10 to 15 minutes more or until golden brown.

THE FAMILY STONE

(2005)

When uptight Meredith accompanies her boyfriend to visit his family for the holidays, things definitely don't go as planned. And when she attempts to reverse her bad first impression by preparing her family's traditional breakfast strata, things go even more poorly. With an all-star case that includes Sarah Jessica Parker, Diane Keaton, Craig T. Nelson, Dermot Mulroney, Rachel McAdams, and Luke Wilson, *The Family Stone* is a perfect watch for you and your family as you enjoy this flavorful casserole.

OVERNIGHT

ORANGE-CINNAMON ROLLS

❋ MAKES 1 DOZEN ❋

Here's another treat that'll brighten up Christmas morning. Although it's not necessary to let the rolls rest in the refrigerator overnight, you may appreciate doing so—that's more convenient than waking up super early to allow the dough enough time to rise before baking.

½ cup warm whole milk or orange juice (100°F to 110°F)

1 (¼-ounce) package active dry yeast (2¼ teaspoons)

⅓ cup granulated sugar

⅓ cup unsalted butter, melted, plus more for greasing bowl and pan

2 large eggs

3 cups all-purpose flour, plus more for dusting

1 teaspoon fine sea salt

Cinnamon-Orange Filling (recipe follows)

Orange Icing (recipe follows)

1. In a large mixing bowl, combine the milk or juice and yeast; let stand for 5 minutes (mixture should appear bubbly on the surface).

2. Add the sugar, butter, and eggs to the yeast mixture. Beat with an electric mixer at medium speed for one minute or until smooth.

3. Gradually add the flour and salt to the yeast mixture; beat until a dough forms (dough will be slightly sticky). Place the dough in a large, lightly buttered bowl, turning to coat. Cover and let rise for 2 hours or until doubled in size. Meanwhile, prepare the Cinnamon-Orange Filling.

4. Punch the dough down; turn out onto a floured surface. Roll dough into a 16x8-inch rectangle. Spread the Cinnamon-Orange Filling over the dough. Roll the dough, starting on the longer side, into a log. Cut into 12 rolls.

5. Place rolls in a lightly buttered 9-inch round cake pan or pie plate. Cover and refrigerate for 8 hours or overnight.

6. Uncover the rolls and let them rise at room temperature for 1 hour. Preheat the oven to 350°F.

7. Bake the rolls for 18 to 22 minutes or until golden. Drizzle the Orange Icing over warm rolls.

ARTHUR CHRISTMAS

(2011)

This delightfully clever British animated film finally explains how Santa, voiced by Jim Broadbent, can deliver billions of toys to children around the world in just one night. Christmas Eve is a night run with military precision, and with the help of cutting-edge technology, all under the watchful eye of Santa's eldest son, voiced by Hugh Laurie. Until one night when things don't go according to plan, and Santa's younger and idealistic son, Arthur, steps up to fulfill the family's annual mission.

CINNAMON-ORANGE FILLING

¼ cup unsalted butter, softened

¼ cup firmly packed light brown sugar

1 tablespoon ground cinnamon

2 teaspoons orange zest

In a small bowl, combine the butter, brown sugar, cinnamon, and orange zest, stirring until smooth and well blended.

ORANGE ICING

½ cup powdered sugar

1 tablespoon orange juice

In a small bowl, combine the powdered sugar and orange juice, stirring until smooth.

HAPATI

→ **SERVES 8** ←

The trick to making these flatbreads flaky and tender is to create a spiral coil with the dough before flattening it into a disk. What makes this recipe different from the chapati that can be found in India is that it uses oil instead of ghee (clarified browned butter). The dough will be sticky and will require a heavily floured surface. Just flour the surface and rolling pin; adding more flour into the dough mixture will toughen it.

3½ cups all-purpose flour, plus more for rolling out

2 teaspoons granulated sugar

1½ teaspoons fine sea salt

1¼ cups water

½ cup vegetable oil

Additional oil or cooking spray for brushing and cooking

1. In a large bowl, combine the flour, sugar, and salt. Stir in the water and oil. (The dough will be very soft and sticky.)

2. Place the dough on a heavily floured board and knead for 7 to 10 minutes. (You can knead for 3 minutes using a dough hook in an electric mixer, if desired.)

3. Divide the dough into 8 pieces and let rest for 15 minutes.

4. On a heavily floured surface, roll each piece into an 8-inch circle. Brush the tops with a very thin layer of oil (for ease, you can spray lightly with cooking spray). Roll each circle into a long cylinder, then curl each one into a tight spiral. Let the dough rest for 15 minutes.

5. On a heavily floured surface, roll each spiral into a circle about ⅛-inch thick just before cooking.

6. Heat a thin layer of oil in a nonstick skillet over medium-high heat. Cook the chapati for 2 minutes until golden brown; flip over and cook for 1 to 2 minutes or until golden and puffed. Repeat with remaining dough. Cover and keep the chapati warm until the remaining are cooked. Best if eaten immediately.

HOLIDAY IN THE WILD
(2019)

Rob Lowe and Kristen Davis star in this sweet and heartwarming film set at an elephant sanctuary in Zambia. Watching the pair hug a baby elephant will have you reaching for your phone to check flights, or better yet, your checkbook to donate toward elephant conservation. Christmas meals in many East African countries celebrate local cuisine, and often feature a hearty goat stew, which is served with unleavened breads called chapati.

Forget White Castle burgers, it's a hot waffle that inspires cravings in this sequel featuring Harold and Kumar, played by John Cho and Kal Penn, respectively, as reunited friends who, once again, get into a lot of trouble. A self-satirizing NPH (Neil Patrick Harris, for those of you not in the know), hawks the WaffleBot, but you can make these fluffy, cinnamon-scented waffles in any waffle iron you have at home.

CINNAMON-APPLE WAFFLES

→ MAKES 8 WAFFLES ←

Waffle batter is similar to pancake batter, but often contains more butter or oil and is heated on both top and bottom to create a crispier texture.

1½ cups all-purpose flour

2 tablespoons light brown sugar

2 teaspoons baking powder

2 teaspoons ground cinnamon

½ teaspoon fine sea salt

2 large eggs, lightly beaten

1 cup whole milk

¼ cup unsalted butter, melted

1 medium baking apple such as Braeburn, Granny Smith, or Honeycrisp, peeled and grated

Melted butter or oil, for greasing waffle iron (optional)

Cinnamon-Butter-Maple Syrup (recipe follows)

Whipped cream, for serving

1. Preheat a Belgian waffle iron.

2. In a large bowl, combine the flour, brown sugar, baking powder, cinnamon, and salt.

3. In a separate bowl, whisk the eggs, milk, and butter. Stir in the grated apple. Fold the egg mixture into the flour mixture, stirring just until combined.

4. If necessary, lightly grease the waffle iron. Spoon ⅓ to ½ cup of the batter into the waffle iron, making sure each segment is filled. Cook for 4 to 5 minutes until golden brown. Transfer to a plate and cover with foil. Repeat with the remaining batter. Serve with syrup and whipped cream.

CINNAMON-BUTTER-MAPLE SYRUP

→ MAKES ¾ CUP ←

½ cup pure maple syrup

¼ cup unsalted butter

½ to 1 teaspoon ground cinnamon

In a small saucepan, combine the maple syrup, butter, and cinnamon. Cook over medium heat, stirring constantly, until the butter melts and the mixture is smooth. Keep warm.

YORKSHIRE PUDDING
WITH HERBS

✦ MAKES 1 DOZEN ✦

Also known as popovers in the United States, Yorkshire puddings are a British treat of high-rising rolls that are crisp on the outside with tender, hollow interiors. The trick to getting the fluffiest texture is to allow the batter to rest at least thirty minutes. The puddings are often served along with roast beef (see recipe on page 101), with the rendered fat being used to grease the cups and add flavor.

3 large eggs

1½ cups whole milk

1½ cups all-purpose flour

1 tablespoon minced fresh chives

1 teaspoon minced fresh rosemary

½ teaspoon fine sea salt

¼ cup melted beef or duck fat, oil, or clarified butter

1. In a medium bowl, combine the eggs and milk, whisking until well blended. Whisk in the flour, chives, rosemary, and salt. Let stand for at least 30 minutes or until the mixture is room temperature.

2. Place the oven rack to just above the center. Preheat the oven to 450°F.

3. Place a 12-cup popover or muffin pan in the oven and preheat for 5 minutes.

4. Carefully remove the pan from the oven and brush the fat evenly in the center and along the sides.

5. Stir the batter if separated, and pour it evenly among the preheated cups.

6. Bake for 10 minutes. Reduce the oven to 325°F and bake for 20 minutes more or until golden brown and puffed. Serve immediately.

LOVE ACTUALLY
(2003)

Love it or hate it, this bittersweet holiday movie set in London, England, which explores complex feelings in several different romantic relationships and friendships, is one of the most well-known modern holiday films. With a stellar ensemble cast that includes Hugh Grant, Emma Thompson, Laura Linney, Liam Neeson, Alan Rickman, and more, *Love Actually* is sure to inspire any viewer to cook up some British cuisine.

APPETIZERS & SOUPS

PIGS IN A BLANKET

⇒ MAKES ABOUT 3½ DOZEN ⇐

Upscale cooked sausages come in a variety of flavors, but you can use plain hot dogs for a basic wrap. Freezing the pieces after they are assembled and sliced helps them bake evenly.

½ cup coarse-grain Dijon mustard, divided

⅓ cup bacon jam, pepper jelly, or orange marmalade

1 (17.3-ounce) package frozen puff pastry, thawed

Flour, for dusting

2 (12-ounce or 4-link) packages chicken-and-apple or other cooked sausage

1 large egg, lightly beaten

3 tablespoons everything bagel seasoning or other salt-free seasoning blend

1. In a small bowl, combine ¼ cup of the mustard with the jam. Cover and refrigerate until ready to serve.

2. On a floured surface, roll out the puff pastry. Cut pastry dough into 4 rectangles. Lightly spread or brush half of each rectangle with the remaining ¼ cup mustard. Place the sausages along the mustard-brushed edges and roll up, pressing the seams to seal.

3. Brush the rolls with the egg and sprinkle evenly with the bagel seasoning. Cut each roll diagonally into five pieces. Freeze for 30 minutes.

4. Preheat the oven to 400°F. Line a baking sheet with parchment paper, nonstick foil, or a silicone baking mat.

5. Arrange the pigs in a blanket on the prepared pan. Bake for 20 to 25 minutes or until golden brown. Serve with the mustard-jam dipping sauce.

SHREK THE HALLS

(2007)

Shrek, Donkey, and Fiona are back at it again in this cute holiday story that celebrates the family made by you or for you. Inspiration for this appetizer comes from the Three Little Pigs who memorably steal a scene when the trio makes fun of themselves for literally being wrapped up in a blanket.

RISE OF THE GUARDIANS

(2012)

Some might argue that this clever animated film starring the voices of Chris Pine, Hugh Jackman, Isla Fisher, Alec Baldwin, and Jude Law isn't exactly a Christmas movie. However, it's set in winter and Santa Claus is a main character, allowing it to pass muster for a family night viewing party during the holiday season, as well as year-round.

GUACAMOLE-STUFFED EGGS

⤞ MAKES 2 DOZEN ⤝

To give the Easter Bunny a bit of recognition but still keep the dish Christmasy, try these tasty stuffed eggs with the traditional holiday colors of red and green. Avocado gives the yolks a muted green color and a more savory flavor. For the brightest effect, add a drop of green food coloring to the filling.

1 dozen large eggs	1 teaspoon hot sauce
2 small ripe avocados, pitted and diced	1 teaspoon ground cumin
¼ cup mayonnaise	1 teaspoon fine sea salt
¼ teaspoon lime zest	Fresh cilantro or parsley leaves, for garnish
2 tablespoons fresh lime juice	½ roasted red bell pepper, chopped, for garnish

1. Place the eggs in a large saucepan and cover with at least 2 inches of cold water. Bring to a boil over high heat. Cover and remove from heat. Let stand for 12 minutes. Drain and rinse in cold water until cool enough to handle.

2. Peel the eggs and cut in half lengthwise. Transfer the yolks to a medium bowl. Cover the whites with plastic wrap and set aside.

3. Add the avocado to the yolks and mash with a fork until very smooth. Stir in the mayonnaise, lime zest, lime juice, hot sauce, cumin, and salt. (For the smoothest filling, process in a food processor.) Spoon or pipe the avocado mixture into the centers of the egg whites. Garnish with the cilantro leaves and roasted bell pepper.

Brown Sugar-Cured Salmon
WITH ZESTY MUSTARD SAUCE

→ **SERVES 12** ←

Try this sweet-and-salty cured salmon thinly sliced and layered over crème fraîche or mascarpone spread on crisp bread.

1 (1½ to 1¾-pound) sockeye salmon fillet

½ cup kosher salt

½ cup firmly packed light brown sugar

⅓ cup chopped fresh dill

1 tablespoon coarse ground or cracked black pepper

1 tablespoon vodka

Zesty Mustard Sauce (recipe follows)

1. Remove any pin bones from the salmon. If salmon was sold packaged or frozen, place the salmon, uncovered and skin side down, in the refrigerator for 2 hours or until the surface is dry.

2. In a medium bowl, combine the salt, brown sugar, dill, pepper, and vodka. Spoon half of the salt mixture in a glass or ceramic 13x9-inch baking dish. Place the salmon, skin side down, on the salt mixture. Spread the remaining salt mixture over the salmon.

3. Cover the baking dish with plastic wrap. Place a dish or small cutting board over the plastic wrap and weigh down with about three cans, such as canned tomatoes or beans, or something of approximate weight.

4. Refrigerate for 12 hours. Remove the weights and plastic; turn fish over, basting with the accumulated liquid. Cover and replace the weights and refrigerate for another 12 hours.

5. Uncover and rinse the fish; pat dry with paper towels. Slice the fish at a diagonal to create ⅛-inch slices; pull slices away from the skin with the knife as you cut and discard the skin. Cover and store in the refrigerator for 3 days or freeze up to 1 month.

TRADING PLACES
(1983)

When a pair of greedy brothers, played by Ralph Bellamy and Don Ameche, engage in a wager to see if reversing the situations of a wealthy commodities broker (Dan Aykroyd) and a street hustler (Eddie Murphy) results in switched behaviors, things don't quite go according to plan. At his lowest point, Aykroyd's character drunkenly crashes his former employer's Christmas party, stuffing a large salmon fillet into the front of his Santa suit to later be eaten while riding public transit.

A fun bit of trivia: At the time *Trading Places* was produced, insider trading on commodities (like orange juice) wasn't illegal. Called the "Eddie Murphy Rule," a part of the 2010 Dodd-Frank financial regulation overhaul prohibits using "nonpublic information misappropriated from a government source."

ZESTY MUSTARD SAUCE

MAKES ²/₃ CUP

¼ cup sour cream

3 tablespoons granulated
sugar

1 tablespoon chopped fresh
dill

3 tablespoons Dijon mustard

2 tablespoons white wine
vinegar

2 teaspoons grated white or
sweet onion

1 teaspoon prepared
horseradish

In a small bowl, combine the sour cream, sugar, dill, mustard, vinegar, onion, and horseradish.

Seafood & Sausage Gumbo

⇥ MAKES 12 CUPS ⇤

Roux, the golden to dark-brown flour-and-oil combo, gives gumbo a thick texture and rich flavor. Be patient—it takes a while to reach the dark mahogany color. Feel free to substitute crawfish for the shrimp and oysters for the crabmeat. You can even add pieces of fish fillets, but add at the last minute and stir gently.

¾ cup vegetable oil

¾ cup all-purpose flour

2 white or yellow onions, finely chopped

2 celery stalks, finely chopped

1 red bell pepper, finely chopped

1 green bell pepper, finely chopped

6 garlic cloves, minced

1½ tablespoons Cajun seasoning blend

6 cups shrimp, seafood, or chicken broth

2 tablespoons tomato paste

1 tablespoon Worcestershire sauce

12 ounces andouille sausage, sliced

2 pounds uncooked medium shrimp, peeled and deveined

1 cup (about ½ pound) cooked crabmeat

3 green onions, sliced

Hot cooked rice, for serving

Hot sauce, for serving (optional)

1. Heat the oil in a large soup pot over medium heat. Whisk in the flour. Cook, whisking frequently, for 20 to 30 minutes until the mixture is dark brown.

2. Stir in the onions, celery, and bell peppers. Cook, stirring frequently, for 10 minutes or until the vegetables are tender. Add the garlic and Cajun seasoning; cook for 2 minutes, stirring constantly. Gradually stir in the broth, tomato paste, and Worcestershire sauce. Stir in the sausage. Bring the mixture to a boil, reduce heat to medium-low, and simmer for 30 minutes.

3. Stir in the shrimp and cook for 10 minutes or until cooked through. Stir in the crab and cook for 2 minutes or until hot. Stir in the green onions. Serve with hot cooked rice and hot sauce, if desired.

THIS CHRISTMAS

(2007)

It's been four years since Ma'Dere Whitfield, played by Loretta Devine, last had all six of her children (Idris Elba, Regina King, Laz Alonso, Sharon Leal, Columbus Short, Lauren London, and Chris Brown) together at home for Christmas. Many dramatic moments unfold as each of the characters struggles with personal crisis, while music and food play pivotal roles. A few of the siblings grab a card from the recipe box and together they cook up a batch of gumbo. The recipe's spicy ingredients symbolize the varied personalities of every member of the family that blend well to make a delicious dish.

(1964)

A skinny Santa Claus? Not on Mrs. Claus's watch! At the beginning of the Rankin-Bass stop-motion classic *Rudolph the Red-Nosed Reindeer*, Santa is so stressed by the day-to-day running of his North Pole workshop that he forgets to eat! Luckily the trusty Mrs. Claus is there to help him out, presenting Santa with hearty soups and stews as she implores him to "Eat, Papa, eat!" This rich and creamy chicken, broccoli, and cheddar soup can warm you through any holiday night.

Chicken, Broccoli & Cheddar Soup

⭢ MAKES 8 CUPS ⭠

Shred a block of cheese rather than buying it packaged. Preshredded cheese has a light coating of starch to keep it from sticking together but also prevents it from melting smoothly.

5 tablespoons salted butter	½ teaspoon freshly ground black pepper
1 yellow or white onion, chopped	¼ teaspoon dry mustard
2 small carrots, julienned or shredded	⅛ teaspoon cayenne pepper
¼ cup all-purpose flour	6 cups (1½ pounds) small broccoli florets
2 cups chicken or vegetable broth	2 cups shredded rotisserie or cooked chicken
2 cups half-and-half	8 ounces (2 cups) freshly shredded sharp cheddar cheese
½ teaspoon fine sea salt	

1. In a large pot, melt the butter over medium heat. Add the onion and carrots. Cook, stirring frequently, for 10 minutes until the vegetables are tender. Sprinkle the vegetables with the flour. Cook, stirring constantly, for 2 to 3 minutes until flour is cooked and very light golden brown.

2. Stir in the broth and half-and-half, salt, pepper, dry mustard, and cayenne. Stir in the broccoli. Bring the mixture to a boil, reduce heat, and simmer for 15 to 20 minutes or until the broccoli is tender.

3. Stir in the chicken and cheese. Cook, stirring frequently, for 5 minutes or until the cheese melts and the soup is heated through.

Kris Kringle
151 W 34th Street
New York NY

ERWTENSOEP
(DUTCH SPLIT PEA SOUP)

→ **MAKES 8 CUPS** ←

This hearty soup, also called "snert," is one of the most well-known winter meals in the Netherlands. It's recommended that the soup be cooked down so thick that a wooden spoon can stand straight up when placed in the center. However, you can adjust the consistency by adding broth if the soup is too thick for your liking.

1 (1-pound) bag dried green split peas

8 cups chicken broth

1 pound pork spareribs or bone-in pork chops

3 slices thick-cut bacon, chopped

1 white or yellow onion, chopped

¼ teaspoon freshly ground black pepper

⅛ teaspoon ground cloves

2 carrots, chopped

1 large Yukon gold potato, peeled and cubed

1 celeriac (celery root), chopped, or 1 cup chopped celery

1 leek, rinsed well and chopped

1 (6-ounce) smoked sausage, sliced

Sliced rye or pumpernickel bread, warmed, for serving

1. Rinse the dried split peas in a wire mesh strainer and place in a Dutch oven or large soup pot. Add the broth, spareribs, bacon, onion, pepper, and cloves. Bring the mixture to a boil, reduce heat, and simmer over low heat, uncovered, for 60 minutes, stirring occasionally. Scoop off any foam that rises to the surface.

2. Remove the spareribs from the pot. Pull any meat from the bones, coarsely chop, and return to the soup.

3. Add the carrots, potato, celeriac, and leeks. Bring to a boil, reduce heat to medium, and simmer, stirring occasionally, for 45 minutes or until the vegetables are tender.

4. Add the sliced sausage to the soup and simmer for 15 minutes or until heated through. Spoon into bowls and serve with warm bread.

MIRACLE ON 34TH STREET
(1947)

We don't all believe easily. Young Susan Walker certainly doesn't. She doesn't believe that Kris, the kindly Macy's employee currently playing Santa Claus, is in fact the *real* Santa Claus. That is, until she hears him speak Dutch to a little girl who recently emigrated to the United States. Kris and the girl sing a Dutch folk song together, and little Susan finally trusts that he is truly Santa Claus. Spread some of your own faith this year with this warm and hearty split pea soup, a traditional Dutch winter dish.

(2009)

Set in a small Texas town in 1964, *Christmas in Canaan* recounts the friendship between two boys at the beginning of the civil rights movement. Based on the book of the same name by Kenny Rogers and Donald Davenport, the film features Billy Ray Cyrus as a single father who devises the plan that turns the boys from enemies to lifelong friends.

HEARTY VEGETABLE STEW

⇥ MAKES 10 CUPS ⇤

Stew meat is economical but can be tough, so a long simmer is necessary to create the most tender bites. For a thicker texture, lightly mash the potatoes once they're cooked through, and their natural starch will release. The leftovers will taste even better reheated the next day.

3 tablespoons all-purpose flour

1½ teaspoons fine sea salt

½ teaspoon freshly ground black pepper

1 to 1½ pounds boneless beef, such as chuck or other stew meat, trimmed and cut into cubes

2 tablespoons extra-virgin olive or vegetable oil, plus more as needed

1 small yellow or white onion, chopped

1 celery stalk, finely chopped

3 garlic cloves

½ cup red wine or beef broth

1 tablespoon balsamic vinegar

2 tablespoons tomato paste

6 cups beef broth

2 teaspoons fresh thyme leaves or dried Italian seasoning

1 bay leaf

4 red or gold potatoes, peeled (if desired) and chopped

3 carrots, chopped

1 cup frozen green peas

1. In a bowl, combine the flour, salt, and black pepper; add the beef and toss to coat.

2. In a large soup pot, heat the oil over medium-high heat. Add the beef in batches and cook for 2 minutes on each side or until well browned. Transfer the beef to a plate and set aside.

3. Stir in the onions, celery, and garlic. Cook over medium heat, stirring often, for 5 minutes. (If mixture is dry, add 1 teaspoon of oil.) Add the red wine and vinegar. Cook for 1 minute, stirring and scraping the browned bits off the bottom. Stir in the tomato paste.

4. Stir in the broth, thyme, and bay leaf. Return the reserved beef to the pot.

5. Bring the stew to a boil, reduce heat to medium-low, and cover. Cook for 1½ hours, stirring occasionally. Stir in the potatoes and carrots. Bring the mixture to a boil, reduce heat, and simmer, covered, for 30 minutes or until the vegetables are tender. Stir in the peas and cook for 3 to 5 minutes or until thoroughly heated.

EGG DROP SOUP

→ MAKES 5 CUPS ←

A good egg drop soup is all about the broth—make your own or buy the finest you can find at the market. Brands have varying degrees of saltiness, so taste first and season accordingly.

4 cups chicken broth, divided

2 tablespoons cornstarch

1 tablespoon low-sodium soy sauce

1 teaspoon dark sesame oil

½ teaspoon ground ginger

⅛ teaspoon ground white pepper

3 large eggs, lightly beaten

½ teaspoon fine sea salt, or to taste

3 green onions, finely sliced

1. In a small bowl, combine ½ cup of the broth and the cornstarch; set aside.

2. In a saucepan, combine the remaining 3½ cups of the broth, soy sauce, sesame oil, ginger, and white pepper. Cook over medium heat for 5 minutes or until hot. Stir the cornstarch mixture into the broth mixture and cook, stirring frequently, for 2 minutes, or until the soup thickens.

3. Remove the pan from the heat. Stir the soup slowly in a circle while drizzling in the eggs, creating long ribbons of cooked eggs. Add the salt and stir in the green onions.

THE NIGHT BEFORE
(2015)

After years of spending Christmas Eve together, three friends played by Seth Rogan, Joseph Gordon-Levitt, and Anthony Mackie decide to end their years-long tradition with one last outrageous adventure in New York City. Lots of mishaps ensue while they rock their ridiculous holiday sweaters. But before the chaos, the boys need fuel: egg drop soup and other Chinese food.

SALADS & SIDES

Quinoa, Kale & Sweet Potato Salad

— MAKES 10 CUPS —

Kale is nutritious but can be tough to eat when raw. Try crushing or massaging the kale with some oil or dressing to break down the leaves, making it easier to chew. Baby kale can be substituted; if using, just lightly toss with the rest of the ingredients, since it's already very tender.

3 cups peeled and cubed sweet potato (from 1 large)

¼ teaspoon fine sea salt

2 tablespoons extra-virgin olive oil

1 cup uncooked quinoa, rinsed and drained

1½ cups vegetable or chicken broth

10 cups (12 to 16 ounces) chopped curly kale

Tahini Dressing (recipe follows)

1 large roasted red bell pepper, sliced or chopped

¼ red onion, finely sliced

¾ cup chopped toasted walnuts

½ cup dried cranberries

1 cup (4 ounces) crumbled feta or goat cheese

1. Preheat the oven to 425°F. Line a baking sheet with foil.

2. In a large bowl, combine the sweet potatoes, salt, and olive oil, tossing to coat. Place the potatoes in a single layer on the prepared baking sheet. Bake for 30 minutes or until the potatoes are tender and browned. Let cool to room temperature, and cover and chill until ready to assemble.

3. In a medium saucepan, combine the quinoa and broth. Bring to a boil, reduce heat to medium-low, and simmer for 15 to 20 minutes or until the quinoa is tender. Set aside for 10 minutes, then fluff with a fork. Let cool to room temperature; cover and chill until ready to assemble.

4. Place the kale in a large bowl. Drizzle about ½ cup of the Tahini Dressing over the kale. Massage the kale by hand in the bowl or in a plastic storage bag for a few minutes until the leaves soften and darken. Add the quinoa, tossing to combine. Stir in the sweet potatoes, roasted bell pepper, onion, walnuts, and cranberries. Toss gently to combine.

5. Transfer to a serving platter and sprinkle with the cheese. Serve with additional dressing on the side.

LAST CHRISTMAS
(2019)

If you listen to the lyrics of George Michael's holiday tune "Last Christmas," you get a hint at what this sweet tearjerker is about. Starring Emilia Clarke and Henry Golding, this film celebrates the spirit of generosity and community that pervades the season. The screenplay was written by Greg Wise and Emma Thompson (Thompson also appears as Clarke's mother, Petra). Throughout, Petra encourages her junk food–loving daughter to eat heart-healthy meals, and this quinoa salad is tasty enough to turn any veggie-phobic diner into a fan.

TAHINI DRESSING

⅓ cup tahini

⅓ cup water

¼ cup extra-virgin olive oil

3 tablespoons low-sodium soy sauce

2 tablespoons fresh lemon juice

1 tablespoon honey

1 small garlic clove, minced

¼ teaspoon fine sea salt

⅛ teaspoon cayenne pepper

In a blender, combine the tahini, water, olive oil, soy sauce, lemon juice, honey, garlic, salt, and cayenne. Process until smooth and well blended. (Thickness of tahini varies by brand. If thick, add a tablespoon or more additional water to get a pourable consistency.)

INSALATA DI MARE
(ITALIAN SEAFOOD SALAD)

⇢ MAKES 10 CUPS ⇠

Prepare the salad the day before or in the morning so the seafood has hours to marinate in the zesty citrus dressing. Stir well before serving and adjust salt, if necessary.

FEAST OF THE SEVEN FISHES
(2018)

This sweet and funny story centers around the budding romance between a young blue-collar Catholic boy and his affluent Protestant crush. A heavily food-centric film, it depicts the Christmas Eve tradition of a grand meal called the Feast of the Seven Fishes, which many Italian Americans celebrate. This dish is one of many that may be served and includes a variety of poached seafood in a bright lemon dressing.

Lemon Dressing (recipe follows)

4 quarts water

1 cup white wine

1 small onion, quartered

4 garlic cloves, crushed

2 bay leaves

1 teaspoon crushed red pepper flakes

1 tablespoon kosher or 1½ teaspoons fine sea salt

1 pound mussels, scrubbed and debearded

2 pounds uncooked medium shrimp, peeled and deveined

2 pounds bay scallops

1 pound cleaned calamari (squid) tubes and tentacles, sliced

3 celery stalks, thinly sliced

1 roasted or raw red bell pepper, chopped

1 lemon, sliced

½ cup lightly packed minced flat-leaf parsley

¼ red onion, quartered and thinly sliced

1. Prepare the Lemon Dressing; cover and refrigerate until ready to assemble the salad.

2. In a large stock pot, combine the water, wine, onion, garlic, bay leaves, red pepper flakes, and salt. Bring to a boil and add the mussels; cook for 3 minutes or until the mussels have opened (discard any cracked or unopened mussels). Scoop out mussels with a spider or slotted spoon and drain well. Remove the meat from most of the shells (save a few mussels in the shell for garnish). Set aside.

3. Bring the poaching liquid back to a hard simmer. Add the shrimp and cook for 2 to 3 minutes or until shrimp are pink and cooked through. Remove with a spider or slotted spoon and drain well. Spread out on a baking sheet to cool.

4. Bring the poaching liquid back to a hard simmer. Add the scallops and cook for 3 minutes until opaque. Scoop out with a spider or slotted spoon and drain well. Spread out on a baking sheet to cool.

Continued

5. Bring the poaching liquid to a boil. Add the calamari and cook for 30 seconds to 1 minute. Scoop out with a spider or slotted spoon and drain well. Discard the bay leaves.

6. In a large bowl, combine the mussel meat, shrimp, scallops, and calamari. Stir in the celery, bell pepper, lemon slices, parsley, and red onion. Drizzle the Lemon Dressing over the mixture and toss gently to combine. Cover and refrigerate until ready to serve. Garnish with the reserved mussels in the shells.

LEMON DRESSING

✦ MAKES JUST OVER 1 CUP ✦

2 teaspoons lemon zest

½ cup fresh lemon juice

2 garlic cloves, minced

1 teaspoon fine sea salt

½ teaspoon granulated sugar

½ teaspoon freshly ground black pepper

⅔ cup extra-virgin olive oil

Whisk together the lemon zest, lemon, juice, garlic, salt, sugar, and pepper in a bowl. Whisk in the olive oil.

(1995)

Sandra Bullock plays Lucy, a token collector for the Chicago Transit Authority who rescues her crush when he falls on the tracks and is mistaken for his fiancée at the hospital. Lucy spends time with his extended family, including a belated Christmas meal which features very creamy mashed potatoes.

CREAMY MASHED POTATOES

→ MAKES 12 CUPS ←

Buttery gold or waxy red potatoes tend to create creamier mashed potatoes than russet potatoes, which can get mealy or gummy. This recipe uses a blend of both, but it's okay to use just one kind. Peels add nutrients, flavor, and texture and are best when hand mashed. They aren't recommended when using a food mill.

3 pounds Yukon Gold potatoes

2 pounds red potatoes

1 tablespoon kosher salt or 1½ teaspoons fine sea salt, plus more to taste

2½ cups half-and-half or whole milk

¾ cup salted butter

1 cup sour cream

2 tablespoons chopped fresh chives, for serving

¼ teaspoon freshly ground black pepper, for serving

1. Peel the potatoes, if desired, and cut into even-sized large chunks. Place in a large pot and cover with water. Stir in the salt.

2. Bring the potatoes to a boil over medium-high heat. Reduce heat to medium, cover, and simmer for 15 to 25 minutes or until the potatoes are tender but not falling apart. Pour into a colander and drain well. Return the potatoes to the pot and mash to the desired consistency with a potato masher. For the smoothest mashed potatoes, run peeled cooked potatoes through a food mill into the pot or a large bowl.

3. In a saucepan, combine the half-and-half and butter. Cook over medium heat, stirring occasionally, until the butter melts. Remove from the heat. Stir the hot butter mixture and sour cream into the potatoes, stirring until well blended. Season with additional salt, if necessary. Transfer to a serving dish and sprinkle with chopped chives and pepper.

MAIN DISHES

ℙLAIN ℂHEESE ℙIZZA

⇀ SERVES 8 ↽

This pizza recipe makes two pies—just in case your family is divided between plain cheese and meaty supreme! It's best to bake one pizza at a time. If you only want to make one pizza, wrap half the dough in plastic wrap and aluminum foil. Freeze up to three months.

Semolina flour creates an authentic chewy texture and flavor. If you don't have any, use fine corn meal or additional all-purpose flour. If adding additional ingredients such as pepperoni, olives, peppers, etc., make sure doing so doesn't overload the dough; otherwise it'll be difficult to transfer to the stone.

1 (¼-ounce) package or 2¼ teaspoons active dry yeast

1 tablespoon granulated sugar

1½ cups warm water (100°F to 110°F)

2 tablespoons extra-virgin olive oil, plus more for bowl

3½ cups all-purpose flour

½ cup semolina flour, plus more for rolling out

1½ teaspoons fine sea salt

1 (14-ounce) jar pizza sauce

3 cups (12 ounces) shredded mozzarella cheese

1½ cups (6 ounces) grated Parmesan cheese

1. In a large bowl, combine the yeast, sugar, and water; let stand for 5 minutes. Add the olive oil, flours, and salt. Stir for 3 to 5 minutes until the mixture is smooth and forms a soft dough.

2. Turn the dough out onto a surface lightly sprinkled with semolina flour; knead two or three times until the dough is smooth and elastic. Shape the dough into a ball; place in a lightly oiled bowl, turning the dough to grease the top. Cover and let rise in a warm place, free from drafts, for 1 hour or until doubled in size.

3. Punch the dough down and let rise again for 45 minutes or until doubled in size again. Divide the dough into 2 pieces. Let rest 10 minutes before rolling.

4. Place a pizza stone or thick greased baking sheet in the oven. Preheat the oven to 475°F.

5. Sprinkle a pizza peel or cutting board with semolina flour. Roll one piece of dough into a 12-inch circle. Spread half the pizza sauce over the dough and sprinkle with half of the cheeses. Carefully slide the pizza dough onto the hot stone. Bake for 15 minutes until the cheese is golden. Repeat with the remaining dough, sauce, and cheese.

HOME ALONE (1990)
HOME ALONE 2 (1992)

After being sent to his room for fighting over cheese pizza he didn't get to eat, eight-year-old Kevin gets his wish for a bit of "me time" that extends longer than he expected when his large and boisterous family jets off to Paris without him. He spends the next few days defending his home against a couple of bumbling burglars who reprise roles in the sequel, *Home Alone 2: Lost in New York*, where Kevin enjoys his favorite pizza while riding in the back of a limousine touring the Big Apple.

WHITE CHRISTMAS

(1954)

Returning World War II vets Bob and Phil, played by Bing Crosby and Danny Kaye, enlist two sisters, played by Rosemary Clooney and Vera-Ellen, to join their effort to save the Vermont Country Inn run by their retired former Army commander. In one scene, Clooney's character suffers from insomnia, and Bob presents her with a platter of sandwiches, explaining that ham and cheese on rye causes him to dream of a tall, cool blonde (wink, wink).

GRILLED HAM & CHEESE ON RYE

⊹ SERVES 2 ⊹

While the sandwiches featured in *White Christmas* are served cold, this version is griddled, since a hot, gooey-cheesed sandwich sounds about right on a chilly Vermont evening.

2 tablespoons coarse-grain mustard

1½ teaspoons honey

½ teaspoon prepared horseradish

4 slices rye bread

4 ounces Black Forest or honey ham

4 slices Swiss cheese

1 tablespoon salted butter, softened

1. In a small bowl, combine the mustard, honey, and horseradish. Spread the mustard mixture on one side of each piece of bread. Layer two bread slices evenly with ham and cheese. Top with the remaining bread slices. Spread the outside of the sandwiches evenly with butter.

2. Preheat a grill press or skillet until hot. Cook the sandwiches for 2 to 3 minutes on each side until bread is golden brown and the cheese melts.

Written and directed by Sergio Pablos, this heartwarming animated tale features stunningly lush animation and the talented voices of Jason Schwartzman, J. K. Simmons, Rashida Jones, Joan Cusack, Will Sasso, and Norm Macdonald. The plot centers around a spoiled young postman, sent to a remote island village where he works out an arrangement with an initially frightening woodsman, Klaus, to deliver toys to children in exchange for letters. Our fish stick recipe is a nod to Jones's character, a teacher turned island fishmonger.

CRISPY FISH STICKS

⊹ SERVES 6 ⊰

Use any firm boneless fish fillets, like cod, pollock, or halibut, or salmon for a bold flavor. Thin fillets like flounder or tilapia may fall apart when cut into strips.

2 large eggs, lightly beaten

3 tablespoons Dijon mustard

2 tablespoons water

1½ cups crushed plain or flavored potato chips

¾ cup panko bread crumbs

½ to 1 teaspoon fine sea salt

½ teaspoon freshly ground black pepper

½ teaspoon paprika

2 pounds boneless, skinless fish fillets, cut into 1- to 2-inch strips

Homemade Tartar Sauce (recipe follows) or store-bought tartar sauce

1. Preheat the oven to 375°F. Line a large baking sheet with lightly greased or nonstick foil.

2. In a shallow boil, combine the eggs, Dijon mustard, and water. In another shallow bowl, combine the potato chips, bread crumbs, salt, pepper, and paprika. Dip the fish into the mustard mixture, then coat in the potato chip mixture. Place on the prepared baking sheet. Bake for 15 minutes or until golden brown. Serve with the Tartar Sauce.

TARTAR SAUCE

⊹ MAKES ABOUT 1¼ CUPS ⊰

1 cup mayonnaise

¼ cup chopped dill pickles

1 tablespoon fresh lemon juice

1 teaspoon hot sauce

½ teaspoon chopped fresh or dried dill

½ teaspoon Dijon mustard

¼ teaspoon fine sea salt

In a bowl, combine the mayonnaise, pickles, lemon juice, hot sauce, dill, Dijon mustard, and salt. Cover and chill until ready to serve.

Buttermilk Fried Chicken Legs

⇀ SERVES 4 TO 6 ↽

This recipe needs a little time to allow the chicken to marinate—start early so you are not eating too close to midnight! It's worth the wait since the chicken is seasoned and crispy on the outside, and moist and tender on the inside. You can also use chicken thighs or chicken breasts (cut in half to cook evenly since they are large).

GREMLINS
(1984)

If you receive a gremlin for Christmas, you must remember three things—no water, no food after midnight, and no bright lights. Chaos ensues when young Billy Peltzer inadvertently allows the rules to be broken and his gremlin eats fried chicken legs after midnight.

1 quart buttermilk

¼ cup firmly packed light brown sugar

1 tablespoon fresh or 1 teaspoon dried thyme leaves

½ teaspoon cayenne pepper

1½ teaspoons fine sea salt, divided

1½ teaspoons freshly ground black pepper, divided

4 pounds bone-in, skin-on chicken legs

2½ cups all-purpose flour

2 tablespoons paprika

1 tablespoon garlic powder

Vegetable oil, for frying

1. Pour the buttermilk into a large, nonmetal bowl; stir in the brown sugar, thyme, cayenne, ½ teaspoon salt, and ½ teaspoon pepper. Add the chicken, tossing to coat. Cover and chill for 6 hours or overnight, turning the chicken pieces occasionally. Remove from the refrigerator and let stand for 30 minutes before dredging and frying.

2. In a large bowl, combine the flour, paprika, garlic powder, remaining 1 teaspoon salt, and remaining 1 teaspoon black pepper.

3. Set a wire rack on a rimmed sheet pan and place in the oven. Preheat the oven to 200°F.

4. Remove the chicken from the buttermilk mixture, draining any excess. Dredge the chicken in the flour mixture, shaking off the excess. (Let stand while oil heats.)

5. Pour the oil into a large, deep cast iron skillet or Dutch oven to a depth of 1 to 1½ inches. Heat the oil to 350°F over medium-high heat.

6. Place chicken in the oil in batches. Reduce heat to medium and cover. Cook for 5 minutes. Remove the lid and increase the heat to medium-high. Turn the chicken over and cook for 10 to 12 minutes, uncovered, or until golden brown. Remove the chicken with tongs, allowing oil to drain, and place on rack in oven to keep warm. Repeat with the remaining chicken.

(2008)

A travel snafu means Kate (Reese Witherspoon) and Brad (Vince Vaughn) won't be enjoying their holiday trip to Fiji. Succumbing to family obligations, the couple visits their separated parents' homes, meaning they participate in four separate Christmas celebrations. Traditional foods have no place in their nontraditional gatherings, but the gusto with which Brad's brother devours a batch of buffalo chicken wings shows how they are a perfect meal choice for anyone's rough-and-tumble family.

Baked Buffalo Wings

⇾ SERVES 4 ⇽

Get a crispy wing without the mess of deep frying with high-temp roasting and a light coating of this secret ingredient—baking powder. Make sure to purchase a nonaluminum brand of baking powder and check the date on the bottom.

4 pounds chicken wings

1 tablespoon aluminum-free baking powder

1 teaspoon garlic powder

½ teaspoon paprika

½ teaspoon fine sea salt

¼ teaspoon freshly ground black pepper

½ cup hot sauce

⅓ cup salted butter, melted

2 tablespoons light brown sugar

Celery sticks, for serving

Blue cheese dressing, for serving

1. Preheat the oven to 250°F. Place two wire cooling racks inside rimmed baking sheets lined with foil.

2. If chicken wings are whole, remove the wing tip and cut into drumettes and flats. Blot dry with paper towels to remove moisture on the skin.

3. In a large bowl, combine the baking powder, garlic powder, paprika, salt, and pepper. Add the wings, tossing to coat. Arrange the wings in a single layer on the wire rack.

4. Bake for 30 minutes. Increase the heat to 400°F. Turn the wings over and continue to bake for 40 to 45 minutes or until golden brown and crispy, rotating pans halfway through cooking.

5. Meanwhile, make the buffalo sauce: In a small bowl, combine the hot sauce, melted butter, and brown sugar. Toss the chicken wings in the sauce. Serve with celery sticks and blue cheese dressing.

GENERAL TSO'S CHICKEN

⇥ SERVES 4 ⇤

Shaoxing cooking wine, sometimes called Chinese cooking wine, is made from rice and specifically made for cooking, not imbibing. If unavailable, substitute mirin or dry sherry in half the amount. The dried chilies in the sauce add a bit a heat and flavor, but don't eat them. You can also substitute ¼ to ½ teaspoon dried red chili flakes, depending on your tolerance for spice.

- 2 large egg whites
- 2 tablespoons low-sodium soy sauce
- 2 tablespoons Shaoxing cooking wine or 1 tablespoon mirin or dry sherry
- ½ cup cornstarch
- ½ teaspoon freshly ground black pepper
- 1½ pounds boneless, skinless chicken thighs, cut into 1-inch pieces
- Vegetable oil, for frying
- General Tso's Sauce (recipe follows)
- Hot cooked rice, for serving
- 2 green onions, sliced, for serving

1. In a medium bowl, whisk the egg whites, soy sauce, and cooking wine. Add the cornstarch and black pepper, whisking until smooth. Add the chicken, stirring to coat. Let marinate for 30 minutes.

2. In a large, deep skillet or wok, heat ½ inch of the oil over medium-high heat. Carefully add the chicken, in batches, to the hot oil and fry for 2 to 4 minutes, turning occasionally, until golden brown.

3. Add the General Tso's sauce to the chicken, tossing to coat. Serve over hot cooked rice and sprinkle with the green onions.

SCROOGED

(1988)

This take on *A Christmas Carol* modernizes the tale by setting the story in 1980s New York City. Bill Murray plays Frank Cross, a television executive and lead "Scrooge." The theme of hindsight followed by redemption plays out as Frank eventually embraces the Christmas spirit and gets the girl, Claire. When Frank and Claire first meet, they go out for Chinese food. We don't know what they ordered, but General Tso's makes a great first-date meal.

GENERAL TSO'S SAUCE

1 cup chicken broth

¼ cup Shaoxing cooking wine, or 2 tablespoons mirin or dry sherry

1 tablespoon hoisin sauce

3 tablespoons low-sodium soy sauce

2 tablespoons light brown sugar

1½ tablespoons cornstarch

1 tablespoon vegetable oil

3 garlic cloves, minced

1 tablespoon minced fresh ginger

2 tablespoons whole dried red chilies or ¼ teaspoon crushed red pepper flakes

1. In a measuring cup or small bowl, combine the broth, cooking wine, hoisin, soy sauce, brown sugar, and cornstarch.

2. Heat the oil in a large saucepan or wok over medium-high heat. Add the garlic and ginger; stir-fry for 45 seconds. Add the chiles and stir-fry for 30 to 45 seconds until the ginger and garlic are light golden brown (stir constantly and do not allow the garlic to burn). Whisk the broth mixture, if separated, and pour into the wok. Cook, stirring constantly, for 1 minute or until the sauce thickens. Keep warm until ready to serve.

Chicken, Sausage & White Bean Cassoulet

⇥ SERVES 6 ⇤

Traditional cassoulet is a lengthy and time-consuming recipe, often requiring a few days to complete. In keeping with the theme of making the most of your time, this version takes a few shortcuts.

LAST HOLIDAY
(2006)

When Georgia Byrd, played by Queen Latifah, is told she will pass away in a few weeks, she's determined to live the rest of her life in grand style, cashing in her savings for a trip to Prague with a stay at a luxurious winter resort. Georgia's passion is cooking, and meeting the resort's famed chef fulfills one of Georgia's dreams. Not wanting to miss out on any of the daily specials at the upscale restaurant, she orders them all. Intrigued with Georgia's gastronomic gusto, the chef personally prepares the cassoulet for her.

6 boneless, skinless chicken thighs

¾ teaspoon fine sea salt, divided

½ teaspoon freshly ground black pepper, divided

2 tablespoons extra-virgin olive oil

14 to 16 ounces duck, chicken, or smoked cooked sausage, sliced diagonally

3 slices thick-cut bacon, coarsely chopped

1 large onion, chopped

2 carrots, chopped

2 celery stalks, chopped

2 teaspoons fresh thyme

3 garlic cloves, minced

½ cup white wine

3 (15.5-ounce) cans white or cannellini beans, drained and rinsed

1 cup chicken or vegetable broth

⅔ cup panko bread crumbs

¼ cup (1 ounce) shredded Parmesan cheese

2 tablespoons salted butter, melted

1. Preheat the oven to 350°F.

2. Sprinkle the chicken evenly on both sides with ¼ teaspoon salt and ¼ teaspoon black pepper. Heat the oil in a Dutch oven or deep cast iron skillet over medium-high heat. Add the chicken and cook for 7 minutes. Turn the chicken oven and cook 3 minutes until well browned. Transfer the chicken to a plate.

3. Add the sausage to the skillet and cook, turning occasionally, for 5 minutes or until well browned. Remove from the skillet.

4. Add the bacon, onion, carrots, celery, and thyme to the skillet. Cook, stirring occasionally for 7 minutes or until the vegetables soften. Add in the garlic and cook for 1 minute, stirring constantly.

Continued

5. Add the wine to the skillet. Cook, stirring frequently, for 1 minute, stirring and scraping up any browned bits from the bottom of the pan. Add the beans, broth, remaining ½ teaspoon salt, and remaining ¼ teaspoon pepper, stirring well. Stir in the reserved chicken and sausages.

6. In a medium bowl, combine the panko, Parmesan, and butter. Sprinkle the panko mixture evenly over the cassoulet. Bake, uncovered, for 45 to 60 minutes or until the meat is cooked through and the topping is golden brown.

ᚱOTISSERIE ᚲHICKEN

⁂ SERVES 4 ⁂

If you don't own a rotisserie attachment for your grill, no worries. You won't need any special devices to make this roasted chicken. Just cook it in the oven. Rotating the bird halfway through the cooking time keeps the breast meat from drying out as well as helping to brown and crisp up the skin.

3 tablespoons salted butter, melted

1 teaspoon fine sea salt

1 teaspoon garlic powder

1 teaspoon onion powder

1 teaspoon paprika

½ teaspoon freshly ground black pepper

1 (5-pound) whole chicken

1. In a small bowl, combine the butter, salt, garlic powder, onion powder, paprika, and black pepper.

2. Remove the neck and giblets from the chicken and discard. Loosen the skin from the breast, drumsticks, and thighs. Spread the butter mixture under the skin.

3. Tie the legs together with cooking twine and fold the wings back and under the chicken.

4. To grill with a rotisserie attachment on a grill: Preheat the grill to medium-high heat or 425°F. Truss and skewer the chicken according to the manufacturer's directions. Cook for 50 to 60 minutes or until the internal temperature reads 165°F on a thermometer. Remove the chicken and let stand for 10 minutes.

5. To roast in the oven, preheat the oven to 425°F. Lightly grease a roasting pan and place a wire rack in the center. Place the chicken, breast side down, on the wire rack. Roast for 30 minutes. Carefully turn the chicken breast side up. Bake for an additional 20 minutes or until the internal temperature reads 165°F on a thermometer. Remove the chicken and let stand for 10 minutes before serving.

IT'S A WONDERFUL LIFE (1946)

In Frank Capra's classic tale starring Jimmy Stewart and Donna Reed, George Bailey longs for travel, yet he spends his entire life postponing his aspirations by helping others instead. While George is helping to save his company from disaster, his steadfast wife, Mary, goes home to ready things there. There's no kitchen in their fixer-upper, so Mary prepares rotisserie chicken on a spit she devises in their fireplace using a phonograph player and string to turn the chicken.

This epic film is based on true events of Christmas Day 1914 when, during World War I, French, British, and German troops held a truce to celebrate the holiday and honor their fallen. Although each country's contingents were chastised by their higher-ups for commiserating with the enemy, this powerful film depicts our shared humanity during a time of intense bloodshed.

Each country has their own version of a meat pie, based on available ingredients. Although food shortages were common during the war, this version features some of the shared ingredients eaten by civilians and military alike.

CHICKEN POTPIE

⇢ SERVES 6 ⇠

Tinned or canned food was a common ration for the troops. While you can substitute canned vegetables and chicken in this recipe in an effort to empathize with the troops, cooked-from-fresh ingredients offer superior flavor and texture.

4 tablespoons salted butter	1½ cups chicken or turkey broth
3 celery stalks, chopped	1 cup half-and-half
1 onion, chopped	3 cups chopped or shredded cooked chicken or turkey
2 large Yukon gold potatoes, peeled (if desired) and diced	1 cup frozen green peas, thawed
2 carrots, diced	1 (15-ounce) package refrigerated pie crusts or Double-Crust Pie Dough (see page 134)
1½ teaspoons poultry seasoning	
¾ teaspoon fine sea salt	
¼ cup all-purpose flour	1 large egg, lightly beaten

1. Preheat oven to 375°F.

2. In a large saucepan, melt the butter over medium heat. Add the celery, onion, potatoes, carrots, poultry seasoning, and salt. Cook, stirring frequently, for 10 minutes or until the vegetables begin to brown and the potatoes are almost cooked through.

3. Stir in the flour. Cook for 1 minute, stirring constantly. Add the broth and half-and-half, stirring until well blended. Bring to a simmer and cook for 5 minutes or until thickened and bubbly. Stir in the shredded chicken and the peas.

4. Place one of the pie crusts in the bottom of a 9-inch deep-dish pie plate. Add the chicken and vegetable filling and cover with the remaining crust. Fold over the edges and crimp to seal. Make several slits in top. Brush the top evenly with the egg. Place on an aluminum foil–lined baking sheet.

5. Bake for 35 to 40 minutes until golden brown and bubbly.

NATIONAL LAMPOON'S CHRISTMAS VACATION

(1989)

Clark Griswold (Chevy Chase) is at it again, trying to create the perfect Christmas surrounded by his slightly dysfunctional extended family. Not unexpectedly, loads of mishaps ensue, and the holiday dinner culminates with the overcooked, dry turkey cracking wide open.

ROAST TURKEY
WITH POMEGRANATE SAUCE

✦ SERVES 8 ✦

To avoid a "turkastrophe," do not overcook the bird, and use a meat thermometer to monitor the internal temperature. Brining is a technique often used to infuse meats with flavor and moisture. While wet brining works well for small cuts of meat, it's awkward and possibly unsafe to soak an entire turkey, since the solution must be kept below 40°F. Dry brining utilizes all the sweet-and-salty benefits without the liquid. Fresh turkeys are ideal; otherwise, thawing time must be built into your schedule if using a frozen one.

3 tablespoons kosher salt

3 tablespoons dark brown sugar

1 tablespoon dried sage

2 teaspoons freshly ground black pepper

1 teaspoon paprika

1 (12- to 14-pound) whole fresh turkey

2 cups water

2 tablespoons extra-virgin olive oil

Fresh rosemary and sage leaves, for garnish

Orange slices, for garnish

Pomegranate arils, for garnish (optional)

Pomegranate Sauce (recipe follows) or Onion & Sage Gravy (see page 93)

1. In a small bowl, combine the salt, brown sugar, sage, black pepper, and paprika.

2. Remove the giblets and neck from the turkey; reserve for other uses or discard. Place the turkey in a rimmed pan and pat dry with paper towels. Loosen the skin from the breast and thighs without detaching or tearing the skin.

3. Spread 2 tablespoons of the salt mixture under the skin. Sprinkle about 2 teaspoons of the salt mixture inside the cavity. Spread the remaining salt mixture over the entire turkey. Turn breast side down in the pan. Cover with plastic wrap and refrigerate for 12 to 24 hours.

4. Uncover the turkey and turn it breast side up. Spread any salt mixture in bottom of the pan over the top of the turkey. Return to the refrigerator uncovered (this will dry out the skin, allowing it to crisp well when roasting) and chill for an additional 12 to 24 hours.

MAIN DISHES   **90**   THE CHRISTMAS MOVIE COOKBOOK

5. Remove the turkey from the refrigerator and let stand at room temperature for 1 hour. Preheat the oven to 450°F. Place a rack in the lower third of the oven and remove any upper racks.

6. Discard any salt or liquid from the bottom of the pan (it is not necessary to wipe any remaining salt from the turkey). Place the turkey, breast side up, on a roasting rack in a roasting pan. Pour 2 cups of water in the bottom of the pan. Brush the turkey with the olive oil.

7. Transfer the pan to the oven and roast for 30 minutes. Reduce the oven temperature to 350°F. Cover the breast with aluminum foil and continue to roast until a meat thermometer inserted into the thickest part of the thigh registers 165°F, about 2½ to 3 hours. Remove from the oven and tent with aluminum foil. Let stand for 30 minutes before carving (turkey will continue to cook).

8. Garnish turkey with rosemary and sage leaves, orange slices, and pomegranate arils, if desired. Serve with the Pomegranate Sauce or Onion & Sage Gravy.

POMEGRANATE SAUCE

⤳ MAKES 2½ CUPS ⤶

1½ cups pomegranate juice

1 cup chicken broth or pan drippings from turkey

⅓ cup white balsamic vinegar

2 tablespoons light or dark brown sugar

⅓ cup water

2 tablespoons cornstarch

¼ teaspoon freshly ground black pepper

Fine sea salt, to taste

In a saucepan, combine the pomegranate juice, chicken broth, vinegar, and brown sugar. Bring to a boil, reduce heat to medium, and simmer for 10 minutes until reduced by about one third. In a small bowl, stir together the water and cornstarch. Stir cornstarch mixture into the pomegranate mixture. Bring to a boil; boil 1 minute or until thickened. Stir in pepper and add salt to taste.

A CHRISTMAS CAROL

(2009)

Throughout decades and in numerous adaptations, every version of this classic holiday film includes the Ghost of Christmas Present bringing Scrooge to the Cratchit home to witness their Christmas meal, featuring a succulent roast goose. When Dickens wrote his holiday fable in 1844, goose was the traditional Christmas meat, and so is featured here.

ROAST GOOSE

WITH ONION & SAGE GRAVY

⊹ SERVES 6 ⊹

Duck is much easier to find than goose in grocery stores, and this recipe will work for either bird. Duck is usually half the size, so check the internal temperature early. Save the fat drippings in the refrigerator or freezer. It's delicious when you use them to sauté vegetables or fry potatoes. You can also serve the Onion & Sage Gravy with your favorite roast turkey or chicken recipe.

1 (8- to 10-pound) whole goose

1 onion, cut into wedges

1 lemon, cut into wedges

1½ tablespoons kosher salt

1 teaspoon paprika

½ teaspoon freshly ground black pepper

Onion & Sage Gravy (recipe follows)

1. Thaw the goose, if frozen, in the refrigerator (this may take up to two days). Remove the neck and giblets from the inside of the goose and cut away the wing tips; discard or save for other uses, such as stock. Cut any extra skin 1 inch above the neck, and remove any excess fat from the cavity. Rinse and dry the goose. Place the onion and lemon wedges in the cavity. Rub the salt over the outside and inside the cavity. Tie the legs together with kitchen twine. Refrigerate, uncovered, for 8 hours or overnight.

2. Remove the goose from the refrigerator, brush off any undissolved salt, and pat dry with paper towels; let rest for 1 hour.

3. Place the oven rack in lower third of oven and preheat to 375°F. Prick the skin all over at an angle with the tip of a thick needle or a metal skewer, piercing just the skin and fat, not the meat. Sprinkle with the paprika and pepper. Place the goose, breast side up, on a rack in a deep roasting pan. Roast for 1 hour.

4. Reduce the oven temperature to 275°F. Remove the roasting pan and drain fat into a metal bowl or can. Roast for an additional 1½ to 2 hours or until a meat thermometer registers 165°F. For extra-crispy skin, broil for 3 to 4 minutes.

5. Remove from the oven and cover loosely with foil. Let rest for 15 minutes before carving. Serve with Onion & Sage Gravy.

ONION & SAGE GRAVY

½ cup salted butter

1 large red onion, quartered
and sliced

2 garlic cloves, minced

⅓ cup all-purpose flour

2½ cups chicken broth

½ cup white wine

2 tablespoons chopped fresh
sage

½ teaspoon fine sea salt

½ teaspoon freshly ground
black pepper

1. In a saucepan, melt the butter over medium heat. Add the onion.
Cook, stirring frequently, for 40 minutes or until the onion is very
tender and begins to brown. Add the garlic. Cook, stirring constantly,
for 1 minute.

2. Add the flour. Cook, stirring constantly, for 1 minute. Stir in the
broth, wine, sage, salt, and pepper. Bring to a boil, reduce heat, and
simmer for 10 minutes.

SANTA CLAUS IS COMIN' TO TOWN

(1970)

Based on the hit song of the same name written in 1934 by J. Fred Coots and Haven Gillespie, this stop-animation film depicts the genesis of Santa Claus, including a look into how he met Mrs. Claus and how reindeer can fly. While all of Kris Kringle's trials come to a happy resolution, the film's villain Burgermeister Meisterburger remains bitter and mean forever. While he never becomes a good guy, this juicy burger might make up for his evil ways.

BURGERMEISTER PERFECT BURGER

⁓ SERVES 4 ⁓

For the tastiest, juiciest burger, buy the best quality beef, ideally ground in the store. Look for ground chuck or another cut with a ratio of 80 percent lean to 20 percent fat. Most of the fat will render off but provides flavor and moisture while cooking.

2 tablespoons salted butter	1 tablespoon Worcestershire sauce
2 tablespoons extra-virgin olive oil	4 slices smoked cheddar, Gouda, or other cheese
2 sweet onions, halved and sliced	8 slices bacon, cooked crisp
½ teaspoon salt, divided	4 tomato slices
1½ pounds ground beef	4 large lettuce leaves or 1 cup baby arugula
1 tablespoon chili powder	4 brioche or hamburger buns, toasted
½ teaspoon garlic powder	

1. Heat the butter and olive oil in a large skillet over medium heat. Add the onions and ¼ teaspoon of the salt. Cook, stirring occasionally, for 30 minutes or until the onions are golden brown.

2. Combine the ground beef, chili powder, garlic powder, and Worcestershire sauce in a large bowl. Blend very gently with your hands until barely blended (do not overwork the mixture). Divide into four portions and form into patties. Press an indentation in the middle of each patty.

3. Heat a large cast iron or other heavy skillet over medium-high heat. Add the patties and cook for 3 minutes on each side for medium-rare or until desired degree of doneness.

4. Place a slice of cheese on top of each burger and let rest for 1 minute. Layer the burgers with the cooked onions, bacon, tomato, and lettuce inside each bun.

OLD-FASHIONED MEATLOAF

→ **SERVES 6** ←

While a higher fat content adds flavor and moisture to grilled or griddled burger, use lean ground beef in this recipe to keep the oil from puddling around the meatloaf in the pan.

2 cups (about 5 slices) lightly packed cubed whole wheat or sourdough bread

½ cup whole milk

1 tablespoon salted butter or extra-virgin olive oil

1 zucchini, grated

1 small yellow onion, finely chopped

2 teaspoons paprika

1 teaspoon dried Italian seasoning

2 garlic cloves, minced

1 pound extra-lean ground beef

½ pound ground pork, chicken, or turkey

1 large egg, lightly beaten

3 tablespoons Dijon mustard

2 tablespoons Worcestershire sauce

1 teaspoon fine sea salt

½ teaspoon freshly ground black pepper

⅓ cup ketchup

1 tablespoon dark or light brown sugar

1 teaspoon apple cider vinegar

A CHRISTMAS STORY
(1983)

Based on semi-autobiographical short stories by Jean Shepherd, this film follows young Ralphie Parker, played by Peter Billingsley, and his family over the course of a Christmas season in 1950s Indiana.

Sitting down to a family meal of meatloaf, mashed potatoes, and red cabbage, Ralphie's mother coaxes brother Randy into devouring dinner by pretending to be a pig and eating facedown without utensils, disgusting his father, "The Old Man." There's no need to cajole your friends and family—this super-moist meatloaf has loads of flavor. The only trick in this family meal is the zucchini, grated to be well hidden.

1. Preheat the oven to 400°F. Line a 9x5-inch loaf pan with foil.

2. In a large bowl, combine the bread and milk; set aside and allow the bread to soak up all the milk.

3. Melt the butter in a large skillet over medium heat. Add the zucchini, onion, paprika, and Italian seasoning. Cook for 5 to 8 minutes, stirring frequently, or until the vegetables are tender and any liquid evaporates. Stir in the garlic; cook for 1 minute. Cool slightly.

4. Add the vegetable mixture to the bread mixture. Stir in the beef, pork, egg, Dijon mustard, Worcestershire sauce, salt, and pepper, mixing gently just until combined. Spoon into the prepared loaf pan.

5. Stir together the ketchup, brown sugar, and vinegar in a small bowl. Spread the ketchup mixture over the top of the meatloaf.

6. Bake for 55 to 60 minutes, until the meatloaf is cooked through and a meat thermometer registers 160°F. Lift the meatloaf out of the pan, remove the foil, and slice.

ELF

(2003)

Raised by elves at the North Pole after sneaking into Santa's bag as a baby one Christmas, Buddy, played by Will Ferrell, tries to fit in, but his comically large stature fails him. With the support of his adopted family, Buddy heads to New York City to search for his birth father. The star-studded cast includes Zooey Deschanel, James Caan, Mary Steenburgen, Bob Newhart, Ed Asner, Peter Dinklage, Amy Sedaris, and Jon Favreau. (Christmas movie fans may recognize Peter Billingsley from *A Christmas Story* playing lead elf in Santa's workshop.) One of the most iconic moments in a movie filled with laugh-out-loud scenes occurs when Buddy pours maple syrup over his bowl of spaghetti to the horror of his stepmother and the delight of his stepbrother. We suggest skipping the maple syrup and enjoying your spaghetti with traditional marinara instead.

MARINARA SAUCE
FOR SPAGHETTI

→ MAKES 8 CUPS ←

If you don't have access to delicious ripe tomatoes, substitute two (28-ounce) cans of organic whole peeled tomatoes, with or without additional seasonings, and reduce the salt to one teaspoon. Cocoa powder is the secret ingredient that mellows the acidity of the tomatoes. Slow cooking creates a richly flavored sauce, and the recipe works better in a large batch since a small amount could scorch with the long cooking time. The upside is that you can easily freeze the extra sauce and have home-cooked flavor whenever you like.

¼ cup extra-virgin olive oil

2 large, sweet onions, finely chopped

1 (6-ounce) can tomato paste

6 garlic cloves, coarsely chopped

2 tablespoons dried Italian seasoning

2 teaspoons unsweetened cocoa powder

½ teaspoon crushed red pepper flakes

1 tablespoon fine sea salt

½ cup red wine

6 pounds fresh ripe tomatoes, coarsely chopped and seeded

2 teaspoons granulated sugar (optional)

Hot cooked spaghetti, for serving

Freshly grated Parmesan cheese, for serving

Chopped fresh Italian parsley or basil, for serving

1. Heat the olive oil in a Dutch oven or soup pot over medium-high heat. Add the onions. Cook, stirring frequently, for 5 to 7 minutes or until tender. Stir in the tomato paste, garlic, Italian seasoning, cocoa powder, red pepper flakes, and salt. Cook, stirring constantly, for 2 minutes.

2. Stir in the red wine and tomatoes. Bring the mixture to a boil, reduce heat, cover, and simmer over low heat for 45 to 60 minutes, stirring occasionally to break up large pieces of tomato.

3. Remove from the heat and blend with an immersion blender for a smoother texture. Stir in the sugar, if desired. Keep warm.

4. Place the hot pasta in serving bowls. Top with desired amount of sauce and fresh Parmesan, and sprinkle with the parsley or basil.

5. Cool and portion remaining sauce into freezer bags. Place flat on a baking sheet and freeze for up to 6 months.

(1945)

If you aren't hungry when you begin viewing this vintage holiday romantic comedy, you soon will be, as almost every scene involves some discussion of delicious meals. The story begins as a war hero, having been stranded for days on a life raft without food, dreams of the ultimate meal. Not allowed solid food in the hospital, he imagines enjoying a gourmet meal, particularly "a big, thick, juicy steak," as he reads *Smart Housekeeping* magazine.

BIG, JUICY STEAK

SERVES 2 TO 4

Use a spatula or tongs when turning to avoid piercing the meat. Allow the meat to rest for a few minutes before serving—slicing early will let the liquid escape before it has a chance to redistribute through the meat.

2 teaspoons chili powder

2 teaspoons dark brown sugar

1 teaspoon garlic powder

1 teaspoon dried thyme or Italian seasoning

1 teaspoon dried cumin

½ teaspoon kosher salt

½ teaspoon freshly ground black pepper

½ teaspoon smoked paprika

½ teaspoon dry mustard

2 (12- to 16-ounce) prime ribeye steaks, about 1½ inches thick, trimmed of excess fat

1. In a small bowl, combine the chili powder, brown sugar, garlic powder, thyme, cumin, salt, pepper, paprika, and mustard.

2. Rub the spice mixture evenly on both sides of each steak. If desired, marinate in the refrigerator for 8 hours or overnight. Let the steaks come to room temperature for at least 30 minutes before cooking.

3. Preheat the grill to high heat. Place the steaks on the grill and cook for 9 to 12 minutes, turning once, until a meat thermometer registers 120°F for medium rare, or until your desired degree of doneness. Cover the steaks with foil and let rest for 5 minutes (the steaks will continue to cook about 5 more degrees).

GARLIC-&-HERB-CRUSTED ROAST BEEF

✦ SERVES 20 ✦

Forget all the sauces, marinades, and rubs—it's the quality of the meat that creates an outstanding meal. Find a butcher who buys local beef (prime is considered the best grade) and ask them to remove the bones, then tie them back on with kitchen twine. The bones add a great deal of flavor but can be a hassle to remove after the roast is cooked. Once the bones are easily taken off, the roast will cut beautifully into clean slices. Since the roast will continue to cook 5°F to 10°F higher while resting, remove at 118°F to 120°F for the ideal medium-rare final temperature of 125°F to 130°F.

1 (10- to 13-pound, five-rib) prime rib roast (see Note)

10 garlic cloves, minced

3 tablespoons extra-virgin olive oil

2 tablespoons chopped fresh rosemary

1 tablespoon fresh thyme leaves

1 tablespoon kosher or 1½ teaspoons fine sea salt

2 teaspoons freshly ground black pepper

Horseradish Cream Sauce (recipe follows)

1. Trim all but a ¼-inch layer of fat from the roast. Place the roast in a roasting pan, fat side up.

2. In a small bowl, combine the garlic, olive oil, rosemary, thyme, salt, and pepper. Rub the mixture evenly all over the roast. Let stand at room temperature for 1½ hours (a cold roast will not cook evenly).

3. Preheat the oven to 450°F. Roast the beef for 20 minutes. Reduce the temperature to 300°F, then continue to roast for 1½ to 2 hours or until the center of the roast registers 118°F to 120°F for medium-rare (meat will continue to cook when removed from oven).

4. Transfer the roast to a carving board, cover lightly with foil, and let rest for 20 to 30 minutes. (If making the Yorkshire Pudding (see page 43), drain the fat from the bottom of the roasting pan and use to grease the cups.) Slice against the grain in ½-inch-thick slices. Serve with Horseradish Cream Sauce on the side.

HOW THE GRINCH STOLE CHRISTMAS

(1966, 2000)

"Fahoo fores, dahoo dores, Welcome Christmas, Christmas day . . ."

Start humming the Whoville song while you, yourself, carve the roast beast. Serve this succulent main dish (big enough to feed a village of Whos) with the Yorkshire Pudding on page 43. Temper yourself or you'll find your pants, like the Grinch's heart, two sizes too small!

NOTE: If roasting a smaller 4- to 5-pound cut of meat, decrease cooking time to the equivalent of 15 to 17 minutes per pound. The internal temperature will not rise as much, so pull the roast from the oven at 120°F to 125°F.

HORSERADISH CREAM SAUCE

¾ cup sour cream

½ cup heavy whipping cream

⅓ cup prepared horseradish

2 tablespoons chopped fresh chives

2 teaspoons fresh lemon juice

1 teaspoon fine sea salt

½ teaspoon granulated sugar

In a small bowl, combine the sour cream, whipping cream, horseradish sauce, chives, lemon juice, salt, and sugar.

ᗷRAISED ᗷRISKET
WITH ONIONS & CARROTS

→ SERVES 5 TO 6 ←

The flavor of braised brisket improves, so don't be afraid to make it a day or two ahead. Allow the sliced brisket and vegetables to cool to room temperature, cover with a layer of parchment and foil (foil shouldn't touch the meat or sauce), and refrigerate overnight. Reheat, covered, at 350°F for forty-five minutes.

1 (10-pound) whole beef brisket

1 tablespoon kosher salt, plus more to taste

2 teaspoons freshly ground black pepper, plus more to taste

2 tablespoons extra-virgin olive oil

3 white or yellow onions, coarsely chopped

1 pound carrots, cut into 2-inch pieces

5 celery stalks, cut into 1-inch pieces

6 garlic cloves, sliced

2 cups dry red wine

1 (28-ounce) can crushed tomatoes with basil

2 tablespoons fresh thyme leaves

1 tablespoon fresh rosemary leaves

2 bay leaves

1. Preheat the oven to 325°F.

2. Trim all but a ¼-inch layer of fat from the brisket. Rub salt and pepper on all sides. Heat the oil in a large stainless-steel roasting pan (set over two burners) over medium heat. Add the brisket and cook for about 5 minutes on each side until browned. If the brisket will not fit easily in a roasting pan, cut in half and brown each piece separately. Transfer the brisket to a platter. Pour off all but 1 tablespoon of fat from the pan and discard.

3. Add the onions, carrots, and celery to the roasting pan. Cook, stirring frequently, for 5 to 7 minutes or until tender and beginning to brown. Add the garlic; cook 1 minute, stirring constantly.

4. Stir in the wine and cook, scraping up any browned bits from the bottom of the pan. Stir in the tomatoes, thyme, rosemary, and bay leaves. Place the brisket, fat side up, on top of the vegetables.

Continued

THE HOLIDAY
(2006)

Turkey and the trimmings don't appear on the table at Iris's, played by Kate Winslet, or Amanda's, played by Cameron Diaz, houses—houses they switched to escape bad breakups occurring just before Christmas. That doesn't mean the sentiment of cooking for loved ones is forgotten, as Iris prepares brisket as part of a Hannukah feast for her new neighbor and friend.

Place a piece of parchment paper over the brisket and cover with aluminum foil (the parchment prevents contact between the foil and tomatoes).

5. Place in the oven and braise for 5½ to 6 hours or until the brisket is very tender.

6. Transfer the brisket from the pan to a platter or rimmed baking sheet and let rest for 30 minutes. Skim fat from the surface of the vegetable mixture, remove bay leaves, and season with additional salt and pepper, to taste.

7. Slice the brisket against the grain and place back in the vegetable-braising liquid.

Corned Beef & Cabbage

→ SERVES 4 TO 6 ←

Corned beef is made from brisket that has been salt-cured in a seasoned brine. Brisket is a tough cut and requires lengthy cooking time to create a delicious fork-tender meal.

1 (4- to 5-pound) beef brisket with pickling spice packet

5 garlic cloves, crushed

2 white or yellow onions, quartered

2 bay leaves

2 teaspoons crushed red pepper flakes

2 pounds red potatoes, halved

1 pound carrots, cut into 3-inch pieces

1 head green cabbage, core removed and cut into wedges

¼ teaspoon freshly ground black pepper

1. Place the beef, fat side up, in a large stockpot and cover with water. Add the contents of the spice packet, garlic, onions, bay leaves, and red pepper flakes.

2. Bring the water to a boil, reduce heat to medium-low, and simmer for 2½ hours (beef should be tender but not falling apart). Add the potatoes and carrots. Cover and simmer for 30 minutes. Add the cabbage; cover and simmer for 15 minutes or until the vegetables and meat are very tender.

3. Remove the corned beef and let rest on a cutting board. Scoop out the vegetables, discarding bay leaves, and arrange in a baking dish or deep platter. Slice the corned beef and place over the vegetables. Sprinkle with black pepper.

MEET ME IN ST. LOUIS

(1944)

Have yourself a merry little Christmas as you watch this classic Hollywood musical. Starring Judy Garland as feisty heroine Esther Smith, the film recounts a year in the life of an upper-class family living in turn-of-the-century St. Louis. In one memorable scene, the family sits down at an opulent dining room table to a true Midwestern feast, featuring corned beef and cabbage, and the father proceeds to sternly instruct the cook that their family cuts the corned beef, they don't shave it. You, too, will want thick slices of this tasty and tender meal.

(2004)

With their only daughter, Blair, joining the Peace Corps, Luther (Tim Allen) and Nora (Jamie Lee Curtis) Krank decide to take a cruise instead of celebrating Christmas at home. When Blair unexpectedly returns, Luther and Nora furiously backpedal to get ready for Christmas, with Nora frantically searching for a hickory-honey ham, their daughter's favorite holiday dish.

HICKORY-HONEY HAM

⟶ SERVES 8 ⟵

Smoking the ham on the grill gives it extra flavor. Dry wood chips will burn up in seconds, while two cups of damp wood chips will smoke for about thirty minutes. If you prefer to do all your holiday cooking inside (and don't mind missing the smoky flavor), place the ham in a roasting pan with one cup of broth. Bake at 325°F until a thermometer registers 140°F (about fifteen minutes per pound).

8 cups hickory or other hardwood chips

2 large aluminum foil pans

1 (8-pound) fully cooked bone-in ham

¼ cup salted butter

1 shallot, minced

⅓ cup honey

¼ cup dark brown sugar

¼ cup apple cider vinegar

1 tablespoon balsamic vinegar

1 tablespoon whole-grain mustard

1 teaspoon ground ginger

½ teaspoon freshly ground black pepper

½ cup vegetable or chicken broth

1 teaspoon cornstarch

1. Soak the wood chips in water to cover for at least 30 minutes; drain well. Prepare a charcoal, propane, or gas grill for indirect grilling by heating one side to medium and leaving the other side unheated.

2. Poke several holes in one of the foil pans with a metal skewer, a fork, or the tip of a knife and place on the heated side of the grill. Fill with half of the wood chips. Remove the grill grate on the unheated side and place the other foil pan (do not poke holes in it) on the bottom rack. Pour in 2 cups of water. Replace the grill grate over the foil pans.

3. Place the ham on the grill rack on the unheated side, over the pan of water. Smoke for 2½ hours or until a meat thermometer inserted in the center registers 140°F.

4. Melt the butter over medium heat. Add the shallot and cook for 3 minutes, stirring frequently. Stir in the honey, brown sugar, vinegars, mustard, ginger, and black pepper. Cook, stirring frequently, for 3 minutes.

5. In a small bowl, combine the broth and cornstarch. Stir into the sauce mixture. Bring to a boil. Cook for 1 minute, stirring frequently, until thickened. Reduce heat; cover and keep warm until ready to serve.

BABY BACK RIBS

→ SERVES 4 ←

Since the main character is a skeleton, barbecue ribs are a natural choice to gnaw on while watching this quirky movie. Long, slow cooking is the secret to tender, fall-off-the-bone ribs. Wrapping the ribs in foil shortens the cooking time. This recipe uses pork baby back ribs; St. Louis–style ribs are larger and can be substituted, but they will require about an hour of additional oven time. Finish by grilling or broiling to get that delicious, caramelized char on the outside.

1 (4-pound) rack baby back ribs	2 teaspoons garlic powder
¼ cup firmly packed light brown sugar	½ teaspoon freshly ground black pepper
2 tablespoons paprika	½ teaspoon cayenne pepper
2 teaspoons kosher salt	Quick BBQ Sauce (recipe follows) or store-bought barbecue sauce
1 tablespoon chili powder	

1. Remove the thin white membrane, if remaining, from the back of each rib rack (leaving it on creates a barrier that doesn't allow seasoning and sauce to flavor the meat). For easiest removal, pry up the edge with a butter knife (easier on top of the bone) and grasp with a paper towel. Slowly pull off and discard. For easier handling, cut each rack in half to create 4 batches.

2. In a small bowl, combine the brown sugar, paprika, kosher salt, chili powder, garlic powder, black pepper, and cayenne. Rub the blend evenly over both sides of the ribs. Wrap the ribs completely in heavy-duty nonstick foil. Refrigerate for 8 hours or until ready to cook.

3. Preheat the oven to 275°F. Place the rib packages on a large sheet pan (to catch drips that might escape the foil) and bake for 2 hours. Open 1 package and test to see if the meat is very tender and a rib easily pulls away.

4. Remove the ribs from the oven and increase the oven heat to broil. Open the foil and drain excess liquid, if necessary. Brush the meaty side of the ribs evenly with desired amount of the barbecue sauce. Broil for 2 minutes or until bubbly and lightly browned. (Watch carefully because the sugar will burn if broiled too long.) Cut into individual ribs and serve with additional sauce.

THE NIGHTMARE BEFORE CHRISTMAS
(1993)

There's much debate among fans whether Tim Burton's imaginative film is actually a Halloween or Christmas movie. Considering Santa Claus is a main character (and we all see holiday décor in stores in October), we're going to include it here. The award-winning tale follows Jack Skellington, the pumpkin king of Halloween Town, who gets weary of the same ol', same ol' Halloween and becomes enamored with Santa Claus (whose name he hilariously misinterprets as "Sandy Claws") and all thing Christmas. With catchy songs and an unforgettable plot, this film is worth a watch any time of the year.

QUICK BBQ SAUCE

→ MAKES ABOUT 1 CUP ←

½ cup ketchup

¼ cup chicken broth

2 tablespoons Dijon mustard

1 tablespoon Worcestershire sauce

1 teaspoon liquid smoke

In a small saucepan, combine the ketchup, broth, Dijon mustard, Worcestershire sauce, and liquid smoke over medium heat. Cook for 3 minutes, stirring frequently, or until hot.

DESSERTS

Kurt Russell stars as Santa, who, with the help of siblings Kate and Teddy, must save Christmas after his sleigh malfunctions and all the presents are lost. The story begins as the children's recently widowed mother attempts to maintain their family's holiday traditions by herself, including making sugar cookies "with lots of sprinkles."

SUGAR COOKIES
WITH LOTS OF SPRINKLES

⇥ MAKES ABOUT 3 DOZEN ⇤

The yield on this recipe depends on how small or large you cut the cookies. For very intricate cutters, try this trick: Roll the dough on lightly floured parchment paper. Cut out the shapes and remove all the excess dough. Slide the parchment onto the baking sheet.

1 cup unsalted butter, softened

1 cup granulated sugar

1 large egg, lightly beaten

2 teaspoons vanilla extract

¼ teaspoon almond extract

2¾ cups all-purpose flour, plus more for dusting

½ teaspoon baking powder

¼ teaspoon fine sea salt

Royal Icing (recipe follows)

1. In a mixing bowl, beat the butter and sugar with an electric mixer at medium speed until light and creamy. Add the egg, vanilla extract, and almond extract and beat until combined.

2. In a separate bowl, stir together the flour, baking powder, and salt. Add the flour mixture gradually into the butter mixture.

3. Shape the dough into two flat disks. Cover with plastic wrap and refrigerate for 30 minutes.

4. Preheat the oven to 350°F. Line baking sheets with parchment paper, nonstick foil, or silicone baking mats.

5. Roll half of the dough on a floured surface to ¼ inch thickness. Cut with 2- to 3-inch cutters and place on prepared baking sheets about 2 inches apart. Bake for 8 to 10 minutes or until the edges are just beginning to brown. Cool on the pan 5 minutes, then transfer to wire racks to cool completely.

ROYAL ICING

This general recipe will cover the cookies. For piping small detail, reduce water to three tablespoons or increase the powdered sugar to the desired consistency. For a light lemon flavor (great with gingerbread), substitute one tablespoon lemon juice for the water.

4 cups powdered sugar

4 tablespoons meringue powder

4 to 5 tablespoons water

1 teaspoon corn syrup

Food coloring, optional

In a mixing bowl, combine the sugar, meringue powder, water, and corn syrup, beating well. Divide the icing into bowls and tint with the desired food coloring.

Giant Chocolate Chunk Cookies

→ MAKES 2 DOZEN ←

This extra-large cookie bakes at a slightly lower temperature and for longer time than other cookies to make sure the soft insides are completely cooked before the outside burns. Use a good quality bar chocolate or substitute one (ten-ounce) package of dark or semisweet morsels. For more but smaller cookies, roll about two tablespoons of dough per cookie and bake for twelve to fifteen minutes.

1 cup unsalted butter, melted

1 cup firmly packed light brown sugar

½ cup granulated sugar

2 large eggs

2 teaspoons vanilla extract

2½ cups all-purpose flour

1 teaspoon baking soda

1 teaspoon fine sea salt

12 ounces sweet dark or bittersweet chocolate, coarsely chopped

1. In a mixing bowl, beat the butter and sugars together with an electric mixer at medium speed until well blended. Beat in the eggs and vanilla.

2. In a separate medium bowl, combine the flour, baking soda, and salt. Gradually add the flour mixture to the butter mixture, beating until blended. Stir in the chocolate. Cover and chill the dough for 1 hour.

3. Preheat the oven to 325°F. Line 2 baking sheets with parchment paper or nonstick aluminum foil.

4. Scoop the dough using a ¼ measuring cup and place 2 inches apart on the prepared baking sheets, about 6 cookies per pan. Bake for 18 to 20 minutes, rotating pans, if necessary, until golden brown. Repeat with the remaining dough.

5. Transfer the cookies to a wire rack. Serve warm or at room temperature.

THE SANTA CLAUSE

(1994)

High-powered businessman Scott's (Tim Allen) life takes a dramatic turn when Santa falls off his roof and Scott unwittingly becomes his replacement. Scott attempts to hide his new role, but everyone is unnerved by his sudden weight gain and spontaneous growth of white hair and a beard. Instead of ordering a traditional sandwich or salad during a work lunch, Scott orders a plethora of desserts and declares that warm chocolate chip cookies—no nuts—are his favorite. We don't want to disappoint this Santa, so make these giant chocolate chunk cookies and save a few for the big man.

KRAMPUS

(2015)

The Bavarian legend of Krampus is explored in this scary and sometimes morbidly funny film. Krampus is a horrible beast with horns, claws, and a frightening face who comes to snatch away naughty children, but even the adults are not spared in this tale. A star-studded cast including Toni Collette, Adam Scott, David Koechner, Allison Tolman, Conchata Ferrell, and others play a family whose fights instigate their holiday nightmare. Toys and tools become the creature's weapons. Usually benign, gingerbread men animate from the cookie sheets to become ferocious little monsters. You can make yours naughty or nice and have fun biting their heads off!

NAUGHTY OR NICE
GINGERBREAD MEN

⇥ MAKES 3½ DOZEN ⇤

Molasses gives these deliciously spiced cookies a rich flavor that's tempered by a bit of honey. You can substitute honey for the molasses and vice versa, depending on how light or dark and spicy you want your cookies.

1½ cups unsalted butter, room temperature

1 cup firmly packed light brown sugar

½ cup granulated sugar

¼ cup honey

¼ cup molasses

1 large egg

4 cups all-purpose flour, plus more for dusting

1 tablespoon ground cinnamon

2 teaspoons ground ginger

1 teaspoon fine sea salt

½ teaspoon ground nutmeg

¼ teaspoon ground cloves

¼ teaspoon baking soda

Royal Icing (see page 115)

1. In a large bowl, beat together the butter and sugars with an electric mixer until light and fluffy. Beat in the honey, molasses, and egg.

2. In a medium bowl, combine the flour, cinnamon, ginger, salt, nutmeg, cloves, and baking soda. Gradually beat the flour mixture into the butter mixture.

3. Shape the dough into two flat disks. Cover with plastic wrap and refrigerate for 2 hours or overnight.

4. Preheat the oven to 350°F. Line 2 baking sheets with parchment paper, nonstick foil, or silicone baking mats.

5. Roll one piece of dough on a floured surface, about ¼ inch thick. Cut with a 3-inch gingerbread person cutter or other shape. Place cookies 2 inches apart on the prepared baking sheet. Bake for 10 to 11 minutes, rotating pans in the oven halfway through for even baking. Cool for 1 minute on the baking sheet; transfer the cookies to wire racks to cool completely.

6. Repeat with the remaining dough; gently reroll dough scraps. Decorate with Royal Icing.

"Peanuts" Butter Cookies

⊹ MAKES 7 DOZEN ⊹

Use your favorite creamy or chunky peanut butter, but make sure to thoroughly stir it if baking with a natural variety that often separates.

1 cup unsalted butter

1½ cups firmly packed light brown sugar

½ cup granulated sugar, plus more for garnish

2 large eggs

2 cups creamy or chunky peanut butter

2 teaspoons vanilla extract

2½ cups all-purpose flour

1 teaspoon baking powder

½ teaspoon baking soda

¾ teaspoon fine sea salt

1. In a large bowl, beat the butter and sugars together with an electric mixer until smooth and creamy. Add the eggs and beat until blended. Add the peanut butter, beating until well blended, scraping down the sides as needed. Beat in the vanilla.

2. In a medium bowl, combine the flour, baking powder, baking soda, and salt. Gradually beat the flour mixture into the peanut butter mixture. Cover and chill for 30 minutes or until the dough is firm.

3. Preheat the oven to 350°F. Line a baking sheet with parchment paper, nonstick foil, or a silicone baking mat.

4. Roll the dough into 1-inch balls. If desired, roll in additional granulated sugar. Place on the baking sheet and press with a fork in a crisscross pattern to flatten.

5. Bake for 10 minutes or until golden brown. Cool for 5 minutes on the pan or until firm (cookies will be soft); transfer to a wire rack to completely cool.

A CHARLIE BROWN CHRISTMAS

(1965)

It just takes a few notes of Vince Guaraldi's jazzy tune to recognize one of the most popular and enduring holiday specials. Based on the *Peanuts* comic strip by Charles M. Schultz, this memorable tale explores Charlie Brown's search for deeper meaning amidst the over-commercialization of Christmas. Consider this amazing cookie an homage to the characters we've spent a lifetime following.

Put this absolutely stellar musical on your must-watch holiday list. Dickens's London meets steampunk in this clever tale revolving around genius toymaker Jeronicus, played by Forest Whitaker, who loses his confidence, and the granddaughter who brings the joy back to his life. Phylicia Rashad narrates, while Keegan-Michael Key, Ricky Martin, and Lisa Davina Phillip provide more than a few laughs.

CHOCOLATE-PECAN SNOWBALLS

⇥ MAKES 4 DOZEN ⇤

It takes a snowball fight to crack Jeronicus's hardened shell and make him see the goodness left in life. Instead of throwing these at friends, you'll want to toss a few in your mouth! Chocolate lovers can substitute more mini chocolate morsels for the toasted pecans.

2 cups pecan pieces or pecan halves

1 cup butter, softened

¼ cup granulated sugar

2 teaspoons vanilla extract

2 cups all-purpose flour

½ teaspoon fine sea salt

1 cup mini chocolate chips

1 cup powdered sugar, sifted

1. Preheat the oven to 325°F. Spread the pecans in a single layer on a baking sheet. Bake for 5 to 7 minutes or until toasted and fragrant. Cool completely and finely chop.

2. Line 2 baking sheets with parchment paper, nonstick foil, or silicone baking mats.

3. In a large bowl, beat the butter and sugar with an electric mixer until light and creamy. Beat in the vanilla.

4. Add the flour and salt to the butter mixture. Beat at low speed until well blended. Stir in the pecans and chocolate chips.

5. Shape the dough into 1-inch balls. Place each ball 1 inch apart on the prepared baking sheets. Bake for 15 minutes or until very lightly browned.

6. Let stand for 5 minutes or until cool enough to handle. While still warm, roll the cookies in the powdered sugar. Let stand until completely cool. Roll again in the remaining powdered sugar.

White Chocolate-Espresso Shortbread

→ MAKES 4 DOZEN ←

Christmas prep often goes into the wee hours of the night. A bit of espresso in these cookies offers a kick to help you finish stuffing stocking and assembling toys. Try this for a variation: Prepare the recipe, omitting the espresso powder and bake as directed. Dip in the melted white chocolate, and instead of chopped nuts, substitute crushed peppermint candies.

1 cup unsalted butter, softened

⅓ cup granulated sugar

¼ cup firmly packed light brown sugar

1 teaspoon vanilla extract

2⅓ cups all-purpose flour

1 tablespoon instant ground espresso powder

¾ teaspoon fine sea salt

8 ounces white baking chocolate, chopped

1 cup chopped almonds or pecans

1. Preheat the oven to 325°F. Line 2 baking sheets with parchment paper, nonstick foil, or silicone baking mats.

2. In a mixing bowl, beat the butter and sugars with an electric mixer at low speed until well blended. Add the vanilla and beat well.

3. In a small bowl, combine the flour, espresso powder, and salt. Beat into the butter mixture, scraping the sides of the bowl as necessary.

4. Portion the dough and roll into 3x1-inch cylinders. Arrange on the prepared baking sheets 1 inch apart. Repeat with the remaining dough. Bake for 15 to 17 minutes or until lightly browned on the bottom. Transfer to wire racks to cool completely.

5. Place the chocolate in a glass or ceramic bowl. Microwave in 30-second increments, stirring occasionally, until melted.

6. Dip the ends of the cookies in the chocolate, letting excess drip off. Sprinkle the ends in the nuts. Let stand until the chocolate sets.

NOELLE
(2019)

In this delightful modern holiday comedy about defying expectations, Noelle Kringle (Anna Kendrick) is a good sport, supporting everyone's assumption that her brother, Nick (Bill Hader), will take over after their father passes away. The problem is that Nick wants to get out of the family business and teach yoga in the desert. After he goes AWOL, Noelle goes into the real world to find him.

Linzer Star Cookies

⇀ MAKES ABOUT 2 DOZEN ↽

The hollow-star tops are delicate and can fall apart when moving to the baking sheet. To keep their shape, cut a solid star and place on the baking sheet first, then cut out the center.

1 cup unsalted butter, softened

1 cup powdered sugar, plus more for garnish

1 large egg

2 teaspoons lemon zest

2 cups all-purpose flour, plus more for dusting

½ cup hazelnut, pecan, or almond flour

¼ teaspoon ground cinnamon

1 teaspoon fine sea salt

¾ cup seedless raspberry jam

1. In a large bowl, beat the butter and sugar with an electric mixer at medium speed for 2 minutes or until light and fluffy. Add the egg and lemon zest and beat until smooth.

2. In a medium bowl, combine the all-purpose flour, nut flour, cinnamon, and salt; gradually add to the butter mixture, beating just until blended. Shape the dough into two flat disks. Cover and chill for 1 hour or overnight.

3. Preheat the oven to 325°F. Line 2 baking sheets with parchment paper, nonstick foil, or silicone baking mats.

4. Roll the dough out onto a floured surface to ⅛ inch thickness. Cut into shapes using a 3½-inch star-shaped cutter. Cut centers out of half the cookies with a 2¼-inch or smaller star-shaped cutter. Place on the prepared baking sheets about 1 inch apart.

5. Bake the solid bottoms for 10 to 12 minutes or until just the edges are golden. Bake the star-cut tops for 7 minutes or until barely golden; cool on wire racks. Repeat with the remaining dough, rerolling scraps as needed.

6. Spread the solid-bottom cookies evenly with the jam; sprinkle the remaining hollow stars with the powdered sugar. Top each solid cookie with a hollow star.

DIE HARD
(1988)

Yippee-ki-yay! In one of the first action-holiday flicks, Bruce Willis's one-liners are instantly recognizable to those who consider this to be quintessential Christmas viewing. Even though the bad guys spoke German, we're going to celebrate their delicious holiday traditions with this delicious Austrian-German cookie. *Welcome to the party, pal!*

E. T. A. Hoffmann's story "The Nutcracker and the Mouse King" has been interpreted in many forms, from classical ballet to fantastical films such as the *The Nutcracker and the Four Realms*. The story centers around a young girl who dreams of an enchanted world where toys come to life and where she famously interacts with the Sugar Plum Fairy. Like Hoffmann's original "Nutcracker," there are numerous interpretations of sugar plums, which were originally thought to be hard candy and now commonly mean a honey-sweetened dried-fruit-and-nut blend that is shaped into balls and rolled in coarse sugar.

SUGAR PLUMS

→ MAKES 4½ DOZEN ←

Feel free to substitute other dried fruit such as cherries, cranberries, figs, or raisins for the prunes, apricots, or dates.

1 cup slivered almonds	¼ cup crystallized ginger
1 cup walnut pieces or hazelnuts	1 teaspoon orange zest
¼ cup honey	1 teaspoon ground cinnamon
1 cup pitted prunes	½ teaspoon ground allspice
½ cup dried apricots	½ teaspoon ground nutmeg
½ cup pitted dried dates	⅓ cup coarse sugar, such as turbinado, or powdered sugar

1. Preheat the oven to 350°F. Arrange the almonds and walnuts in a single layer on a large baking sheet. Bake for 5 to 8 minutes or until lightly toasted. Cool completely.

2. Place the toasted nuts, honey, prunes, apricots, dates, ginger, orange zest, cinnamon, allspice, and nutmeg in a food processor. Pulse until the mixture is coarsely and evenly chopped, stopping and scraping down the sides of the bowl, if necessary.

3. Spread the coarse sugar on a large plate. Form the nut and fruit mixture into 1-inch balls and roll in the sugar. Place the sugar plums in an airtight container with wax paper between the layers and store in the refrigerator up to 1 month. Remove from refrigerator and let stand at room temperature before serving.

OFFICE CHRISTMAS PARTY

(2016)

The over-the-top antics in this lighthearted and bawdy holiday film starring Jennifer Aniston, Jason Bateman, Kate McKinnon, T. J. Miller, and Olivia Munn make this an adults-only holiday watch. While the plot might not be realistic, large tubs of flavored popcorn sent company-to-company as holiday greetings can be found in almost every breakroom. Enjoy a batch of this homemade caramel corn while you watch the movie and wish you did—or maybe didn't—have a boss like the one on-screen.

CARAMEL CORN

→ MAKES 14 CUPS ←

The popped corn won't fit in a standard large mixing bowl. Use an extremely large one or divide it into two bowls. Once the caramel corn has cooled and is broken into pieces, you can fancy up the mix with candy-coated chocolate or peanut butter pieces, pretzels, smoked nuts, and/or dried cranberries. Keep the caramel corn in an airtight container until ready to serve, since humidity makes it sticky.

16 cups popped corn (about ¾ cup kernels)

1 cup unsalted butter

½ cup light corn syrup

2 cups firmly packed light brown sugar

1 teaspoon fine sea salt

½ teaspoon baking soda

1 tablespoon vanilla extract

1. Preheat the oven to 250°F. Line 2 baking sheets with parchment paper or nonstick foil; set aside. Place the popped corn in one very large bowl or two large bowls.

2. In a saucepan, combine the butter, corn syrup, and brown sugar. Cook over medium heat, stirring often, until the butter melts and the sugar dissolves. Increase the heat to medium-high and bring to a boil. Cook, without stirring, until the mixture reaches 255°F on a candy or digital instant-read thermometer. Remove pan from the heat.

3. Stir in the salt, baking soda, and vanilla (the mixture will bubble). Pour the mixture evenly over the popcorn, tossing gently to coat. Transfer to the prepared baking sheets.

4. Bake for 1 hour, stirring occasionally. Let stand on the baking sheets until completely cool. Break into pieces. Store in an airtight container for two weeks.

Sweet Potato Pie

⇥ SERVES 8 ⇤

While roasting sweet potatoes brings out their sweetness, oven temperatures tend to crisp up the exterior. Boiled sweet potatoes will be very tender, enabling them to mash into a very smooth consistency.

2 large sweet potatoes (2 pounds), peeled and cubed

⅔ cup granulated sugar

⅓ cup unsalted butter, melted

2 large eggs

½ cup half-and-half or whole milk

1 teaspoon vanilla extract

¼ teaspoon ground cinnamon

¼ teaspoon ground nutmeg

½ teaspoon fine sea salt

1 unbaked homemade (½ recipe lattice crust; see page 134) or store-bought pie crust

1. Preheat the oven to 325°F.

2. Place the sweet potatoes in a medium saucepan and add water to cover. Bring to a boil, reduce heat, and simmer for 15 minutes or until the potatoes are tender.

3. Drain the potatoes and let cool to room temperature. Mash with a potato masher or beat with an electric mixer until smooth.

4. In a large bowl, whisk together the sugar, butter, eggs, half-and-half, vanilla, cinnamon, nutmeg, and salt. Add the mashed sweet potatoes, mixing well.

5. Place the uncooked pie dough in a shallow 9-inch pie plate, crimping the sides if desired.

6. Pour the sweet potato mixture into the crust. Bake for 1 hour or until a toothpick inserted in the center comes out clean. Cool on a wire rack.

ALMOST CHRISTMAS

(2016)

The Christmas season is a bit melancholy for the Meyers family as their patriarch, Walter, played by Danny Glover, hosts the holiday alone after his wife's passing. The premise seems sad, but there are a lot of funny moments as the family reunites. One of Walter's goals is to make a delicious sweet potato pie from his wife's recipe, and after much trial and error, he finally succeeds.

(2017)

This thirty-minute animated feature, based on Frank McCourt's short story of the same name, is set in turn-of-the-century rural Ireland. A charming and sweet tale, it shares a child's innocent wish to help others and will inspire any viewer to participate in the spirit of generosity that is at the heart of the Christmas season. Ireland's famed landscape is a beautiful mix of rolling hills and lush green vegetation, so these layered brownies include a Kelly-green mint filling that's a joy to nibble.

THREE-LAYER MINT BROWNIES

→ MAKES 2 DOZEN ←

Start these charming old-school brownies early in the morning or the day ahead since chilling them in the freezer or refrigerator helps set each layer. They freeze beautifully, so you can store some away to serve to carolers or guests who spontaneously drop in.

8 ounces semisweet or sweet dark chocolate, coarsely chopped

1¼ cups unsalted butter

1½ cups firmly packed light brown sugar

½ cup granulated sugar

4 large eggs

2 teaspoons vanilla extract

1 cup all-purpose flour

⅓ cup unsweetened cocoa powder

½ teaspoon baking powder

¾ teaspoon fine sea salt

Mint Layer (recipe follows)

Ganache Layer (recipe follows)

1. Make the brownie layer: Preheat the oven to 350°F. Line a 13x9-inch baking pan with parchment paper or nonstick foil, leaving a few inches to hang over the sides for easier removal.

2. In a large, heavy saucepan, combine the chocolate and butter. Cook over low heat, stirring occasionally, just until the chocolate and butter melt. Remove from heat and stir in the sugars until dissolved. Stir in the eggs and vanilla extract.

3. In a medium bowl, combine the flour, cocoa powder, baking powder, and salt. Stir into the chocolate mixture.

4. Pour the batter into the prepared baking pan. Bake for 30 minutes; cool completely.

5. Spread the Mint Layer over the brownies and refrigerate or freeze until chilled and firm. Spread the Ganache Layer over the chilled brownies and return to the refrigerator or freezer until ganache is firm. Cut into squares.

MINT LAYER

→ MAKES ABOUT 1½ CUPS ←

½ cup unsalted butter

2 cups powdered sugar

2 tablespoons whole milk

1 teaspoon peppermint extract

1 to 2 drops green food
coloring, plus more as needed

In a mixing bowl, beat the butter with an electric mixer until smooth.
Gradually add the powdered sugar and milk, beating at low speed
until just combined, then at medium speed until well blended. Add the
peppermint extract and food coloring, beating at medium speed until well
blended. For a darker color, add another drop of food coloring, if desired.

GANACHE LAYER

→ MAKES ABOUT 1½ CUPS ←

½ cup heavy cream

8 ounces semisweet or
sweet dark chocolate,
coarsely chopped

½ cup unsalted butter,
cut into pieces

Pinch salt

In a small saucepan, heat the heavy cream over medium-low heat
(do not boil). Add the chocolate, stirring constantly, until the mixture
is smooth. Remove from the heat and add the butter and salt, stirring
until butter melts and mixture is smooth.

Young Jessica discovers an injured reindeer she's convinced is Santa's Prancer, even though her struggling, widowed father believes the animal is just a nuisance. Jessica's conviction is contagious, and soon the whole town finds inspiration. In one humorous scene, Prancer escapes the barn and runs amok through the house, devouring the fruit pies set out to cool. If you're like Prancer and don't want to wait, you can eat this Apple & Blueberry Pie while it's still warm along with a scoop of vanilla ice cream!

Apple & Blueberry Pie

⇢ SERVES 8 ⇠

Baking apples, such as Granny Smith, Honeycrisp, Jonagold, Gala, or Cortland, are ideal, since their flavor is superior and they hold their shape when cooked. Try mixing tart apples (like Granny Smith) with a sweeter variety (like Gala) for a delicious blend.

4 to 5 baking apples (about 6 cups), peeled and thinly sliced	½ teaspoon fine sea salt
	¼ teaspoon ground nutmeg
2 cups frozen blueberries, thawed	1 recipe Double Crust Pie Dough (recipe follows) or 1 (14.1-ounce) package refrigerated pie crusts
1 tablespoon lemon juice	
¼ cup firmly packed light brown sugar	1 tablespoon unsalted butter, cut into small pieces
⅓ cup granulated sugar	1 egg white, lightly beaten
¼ cup all-purpose flour	1 teaspoon coarse or granulated sugar
1 teaspoon ground cinnamon	

1. Preheat the oven to 425°F.

2. In a large bowl, combine the apples, blueberries, and lemon juice, tossing to coat. In a small bowl, combine the sugars, flour, cinnamon, salt, and nutmeg. Sprinkle the fruit mixture with the sugar mixture, tossing gently until well blended.

3. Roll one pie crust into a 12-inch circle on a lightly floured surface. Place in a 9-inch-deep pie plate.

4. Pour the fruit mixture into the crust. Sprinkle the top with the butter.

5. Roll the remaining pie crust into an 11-inch circle. Cut into 1½- to 2-inch strips. Place the strips in a lattice pattern over the top of the pie and crimp the edges to seal. Brush with the egg white and sprinkle the sugar on top.

6. Bake for 15 minutes; reduce heat to 350°F. Bake an additional 60 minutes or until golden brown and bubbly. Shield the edges of the crust with foil, if necessary, to prevent overbrowning. Cool on a wire rack.

DOUBLE-CRUST PIE DOUGH

MAKES TWO 9-INCH CRUSTS

2¾ cups all-purpose flour, plus more for dusting

¾ teaspoon fine sea salt

¼ cup vegetable shortening or butter

10 tablespoons unsalted butter, cut into pieces

⅓ to ½ cup ice water

1. In a food processor, combine the flour and salt, pulsing until well blended. Add the shortening and pulse until well blended and finely textured.

2. Add the butter and pulse until crumbly. Do not overmix. The mixture should have lumps of butter the size of peas throughout.

3. With the processor running, gradually add the ice water and process until the dough just begins to stick together. Turn the dough mixture out onto a floured surface and knead gently until it sticks together in a ball.

4. Divide the dough in half and wrap in plastic wrap. Cover and chill for 30 minutes.

MINCE TARTLETS

→ MAKES 2 DOZEN ←

Like this sweet movie, mince pies are a British treat, originally somewhat savory and made with meat and lard. This version is all sweet and made with a delicious blend of dried fruit, fresh apples, and orange zest. They freeze well, but allow them to come to room temperature before eating.

½ cup dried cherries

½ cup dried cranberries

½ cup dried dates

½ cup dried apricots

½ cup raisins or golden raisins

3 tablespoons crystallized ginger

2 teaspoons orange zest

¾ cup firmly packed light brown sugar

½ teaspoon ground cinnamon

½ teaspoon ground nutmeg

¼ teaspoon ground cloves

¼ teaspoon fine sea salt

2 large tart apples, peeled and coarsely grated

¼ cup unsalted butter, melted

2 tablespoons brandy or cognac

Flour, for dusting

Cream Cheese Pastry (recipe follows)

1 large egg, lightly beaten

1. Preheat the oven to 400°F.

2. In a food processor, combine half the cherries, cranberries, dates, apricots, and raisins. Pulse until finely and evenly chopped. Transfer to a large bowl. Repeat with the remaining fruit. Stir in the ginger, orange zest, brown sugar, cinnamon, nutmeg, cloves, and salt. Add the apples, butter, and brandy, stirring until well blended.

3. Roll pastry dough on a floured surface to ¼ inch thick. Cut twelve circles with a 3-inch cutter. Place the circles in two 12-cup muffin tins (or bake in batches), gently pressing dough into the sides. Spoon about 2 tablespoons of the mince filling into each cup. Reroll the pastry scraps and cut into stars, leaves, or another shape. Place shapes in the center of the tartlets. Brush the tops with the egg.

4. Bake for 10 minutes. Reduce the oven temperature to 350°F and bake an additional 12 to 15 minutes or until the tartlets are golden brown. Cool in the pan for 10 minutes, then transfer to a wire rack and cool completely.

GET SANTA
(2014)

In this British comedy, the big man in red—played by Jim Broadbent—finds himself in jail and his reindeer wandering the streets of London after crash-landing his sleigh. Featuring a supporting cast of Rafe Spall, Warwick Davis, and Jodie Whittaker, *Get Santa* will make even the biggest skeptic believe in the magic of Christmas.

CREAM CHEESE PASTRY

2¼ cups all-purpose flour

1 tablespoon orange zest

¾ teaspoon salt

1 cup unsalted butter, cut into pieces

1 (8-ounce) package cream cheese, cut into pieces

1. In a food processor, combine the flour, orange zest, and salt. Pulse several times until blended.

2. Add the butter and cream cheese, a few pieces at a time, and pulse until the mixture forms a soft dough.

3. Shape the dough into two flat disks; cover and chill for 1 hour or overnight.

(1977)

A riverside community featuring Jim Henson's Muppets sets the scene for this reimagined version of O. Henry's "The Gift of the Magi." Emmet Otter and his widowed mother live simply in Frogtown Hollow, each taking on odd jobs to make ends meet. One way Ma earns money is to make pumpkin pies that she sells to buy ingredients to make more pies. These tarts are as sweet as the movie, and their size just as adorable.

Spiced Pumpkin Tarts

→ MAKES 1½ DOZEN ←

For decorative edges, use a 3½- to 4-inch flower cutter. If making ahead for a party, store in an airtight container with wax paper between the layers and freeze for up to two months.

2 large eggs

1 (15-ounce) can pumpkin (not pumpkin pie filling)

¼ cup granulated sugar

⅓ cup lightly packed light brown sugar

1½ teaspoons ground cinnamon

¾ teaspoon ground ginger

½ teaspoon fine sea salt

⅛ teaspoon ground cloves

¾ cup half-and-half or whole milk

1 teaspoon vanilla extract

Flour, for dusting

1 (14.1-ounce) package refrigerated pie crust or homemade pastry for two crusts (see page 134)

Whipped cream, for serving

1. Preheat the oven to 350°F.

2. In a small bowl, whisk together the eggs, pumpkin, sugars, cinnamon, ginger, salt, and cloves. Whisk in the half-and-half and vanilla.

3. Unroll the pastry on a lightly floured surface. Cut into circles with a 3½- to 4-inch round cutter. Fit the circles into a greased 12-cup muffin pan, pressing down and into the sides. Reroll scraps and cut, if necessary.

4. Spoon the pumpkin mixture evenly into each pie cup.

5. Bake for 30 minutes or until the center is set and edges are golden brown. Cool for 10 minutes in the pan. Run a knife around the edges, remove from the pan, and cool on a wire rack. Serve with whipped cream.

A CHRISTMAS CAROL

(1938)

As the most adapted holiday tale, *A Christmas Carol* deserves a second entry in our book. The highlight of the Cratchit Christmas meal is the presentation of the Christmas pudding. Bringing the flaming dessert to the table, Mrs. Cratchit is honored with applause and affection from her family. The pudding is symbolic since, although it is small, it was made well and with great love. A traditional English holiday dish, Christmas pudding is prepared weeks in advance not only to allow the flavors to develop but because the time it takes to cook is quite lengthy. "Now bring us some figgy pudding . . ."

CHRISTMAS PUDDING

⊰ SERVES 8 ⊱

This old-fashioned dessert appears small, but its richness allows for several servings. Steaming the pudding for hours creates an extra-moist dessert. Make sure the water doesn't completely evaporate during the lengthy cooking time. This is especially important if you are using a ceramic pudding mold. If you don't have a pudding basin or mold, use a heatproof bowl or metal Bundt pan small enough to fit in a soup pot without touching the sides.

½ cup raisins

½ cup golden raisins

½ cup currants or dried cranberries

1 tablespoon crystallized ginger, finely chopped

2 tablespoons candied orange peel, chopped

2 tablespoons candied lemon peel, chopped

½ cup brandy, divided

1 baking apple such as Granny Smith or Gala, peeled and grated

6 tablespoons unsalted butter, melted, plus more for greasing

1 tablespoon molasses

2 large eggs

¾ cup fresh bread crumbs

½ cup firmly packed light or dark brown sugar

¼ cup all-purpose flour

¼ cup almond flour or finely ground almonds

1 teaspoon ground cinnamon

½ teaspoon ground nutmeg

¼ teaspoon baking powder

¼ teaspoon fine sea salt

¼ teaspoon ground cloves

1. In a large bowl, combine the raisins, golden raisins, currants, ginger, orange peel, lemon peel, and ¼ cup brandy. Cover and let sit overnight.

2. Stir the apple, butter, molasses, and eggs into the raisin mixture.

3. In a medium bowl, combine the bread crumbs, brown sugar, all-purpose flour, almond flour, cinnamon, nutmeg, baking powder, salt, and cloves. Stir the bread-crumb mixture into the fruit mixture (batter will be stiff and sticky).

4. Butter a 1-liter (4-cup) pudding basin or mold very generously. Spoon the batter into the mold, pressing down to remove any air bubbles and smoothing the top.

5. Cut a circle out of parchment paper the same diameter as the top of the pudding. Generously butter on one side and place, butter side down, on the pudding. Layer two pieces of parchment and two pieces of aluminum foil that are 3 to 4 inches wider than the top on a flat surface. Create a 1-inch pleat in the top (this will allow for expansion as the pudding cooks). If using a Bundt-style pan with a hole in the center, wrap foil on the bottom to prevent water and steam from boiling through the center into the cake. Secure the layers to the top of the mold with kitchen twine. If pudding mold comes with a water-tight lid, use the circle of parchment but omit the parchment and foil layers.

6. Place a trivet or steaming rack in the bottom of a soup pot (to prevent bottom of pudding mold from directly touching the bottom of the pot). Determine how much water is necessary to reach halfway up the pudding mold by placing the mold on the trivet and carefully pouring in the water. Remove the mold and bring the water to a low boil, then reduce heat to a low simmer. Carefully place the pudding mold on the trivet. Cover and steam the pudding for 5 hours over low heat. Check periodically and add more water, if necessary.

7. Carefully lift the mold out of the water and place on a wire rack. Remove the foil and parchment layers and cool completely. Cover the top with a new piece of buttered parchment and wrap with foil. Refrigerate until ready to serve.

8. To reheat, repeat the steaming process for 1 to 2 hours or until heated through. If using a ceramic pudding mold, you can reheat it in the microwave. Remove any foil and cover with a plate or plastic wrap. Cook at 50 percent power for 7 to 10 minutes or until heated through.

9. Remove any parchment or foil and place a serving plate on top of pudding; invert and remove the mold. To flame the pudding, heat the remaining ¼ cup brandy in a small saucepan just until hot (do not boil). Pour the brandy over the top of the pudding and immediately light with a long match or lighter.

In this classic animated film based on the song of the same name, the titular Frosty tells the children he'll come back each year. Indeed, you can find this film consistently shown every holiday season, as Frosty enchants a new generations of holiday film lovers.

RED VELVET CUPCAKES

⇥ MAKES 2 DOZEN ⇤

Red velvet cake makes a cheerful and colorful base for a frosted cupcake. Unlike Frosty, the soft, creamy icing won't melt right away.

1 cup unsalted butter

1½ cups granulated sugar

3 large eggs

1 teaspoon vanilla extract

1 (1-ounce) bottle red food coloring

1 tablespoon white vinegar

2½ cups all-purpose flour

2 tablespoons cocoa powder

1 teaspoon baking soda

½ teaspoon fine sea salt

1 cup buttermilk

Cream Cheese Frosting
(recipe follows)

1. Preheat the oven to 350°F. Line a 24-cup muffin pan with paper liners.

2. Beat the butter and sugar together with an electric mixer until light and creamy. Beat in the eggs, vanilla, food coloring, and vinegar.

3. Combine the flour, cocoa, baking soda, and salt. Add the flour mixture to the butter mixture, alternating with the buttermilk. Pour the batter into the prepared muffin cups, filling about ¾ full.

4. Bake for 18 to 20 minutes or until a wooden pick inserted in the centers comes out clean. Cool completely on a wire rack.

5. Spread or pipe the Cream Cheese Frosting on the cupcakes.

CREAM CHEESE FROSTING

⇥ MAKES 5 CUPS ⇤

2 (8-ounce) packages cream cheese, softened

¾ cup unsalted butter, softened

⅛ teaspoon fine sea salt, optional

3½ cups powdered sugar

2 teaspoons vanilla extract

In a large bowl, beat the cream cheese, butter, and salt, if using, with an electric mixer until fluffy. Add the powdered sugar 1 cup at a time, mixing on slow speed to incorporate, then increasing speed. Beat in the vanilla.

Angel Food Cake

⇒ SERVES 12 ⇐

There's zero fat in this light and fluffy cake, so enjoy it guilt-free! Let the egg whites stand until they get to room temperature, since cold eggs don't whip up as high.

12 large egg whites, at room temperature

¼ teaspoon fine sea salt

1 teaspoon vanilla extract

¼ teaspoon almond extract

¾ teaspoon cream of tartar

1 cup granulated sugar

1 cup cake flour, sifted

Powdered sugar, for garnish

1. Preheat the oven to 350°F.

2. In a large bowl, beat the egg whites and salt with an electric mixer at high speed for 1 to 2 minutes or until foamy. Beat in the vanilla and almond extracts. Add the cream of tartar; beat until soft peaks form.

3. Add the sugar into the egg mixture, a few tablespoons at a time, beating until stiff peaks form.

4. Fold in the flour, ¼ cup at a time. Pour the batter into an ungreased 10-inch tube pan, spreading evenly. Break air pockets by cutting through batter with a knife.

5. Bake for 20 to 25 minutes or until a toothpick inserted in the center comes out clean.

6. Invert pan on a wire rack; cool completely. Run a knife around the sides of the pan to loosen the cake from the sides of the pan and turn out onto a plate.

THE BISHOP'S WIFE
(1947)
THE PREACHER'S WIFE
(1996)

In both the old Hollywood classic, *The Bishop's Wife* (starring Loretta Young, Cary Grant, and David Niven), and the 1990s remake titled *The Preacher's Wife* (starring Whitney Houston, Denzel Washington, and Courtney B. Vance), an angel is sent to earth to help a well-meaning man of God rediscover his priorities. Despite some trials and turmoil along the way in each, both end at Christmas with a happily ever after.

You might not expect *Lethal Weapon* to be labeled a Christmas movie, but since the film centers on the themes of family, overcoming evil, and symbolic gifts, it fits the bill. And after all, the movie opens with the classic tune "Jingle Bell Rock." Starring Danny Glover and Mel Gibson, the film is centered around the relationship of two LAPD partners. Early in the movie, one officer's family celebrates his birthday by bringing him a three-layer frosted cake alit with fifty candles while he is relaxing in the tub. Tasty and sweet, this cake can also be enjoyed at a table, on a couch, or even in your own tub—we won't judge!

THREE-LAYER EGGNOG CAKE

⟶ SERVES 12 ⟵

The flavor of the cake isn't evident in the film, but adding an eggnog-inspired spice such as nutmeg and a wee bit of rum in the frosting gives the dessert some holiday flair.

Cooking spray

¾ cup unsalted butter, room temperature

¾ cup granulated sugar

¾ cup firmly packed light brown sugar

3 large eggs

⅓ cup canola or vegetable oil

1 tablespoon vanilla extract

3 cups cake or all-purpose flour, plus more for the pans

2 teaspoons baking powder

¾ teaspoon ground nutmeg, plus more for garnish

½ teaspoon ground cinnamon

½ teaspoon baking soda

½ teaspoon fine sea salt

1½ cups eggnog, buttermilk, or whole milk

Cream Cheese Frosting (see page 144)

1 teaspoon rum extract

1. Preheat the oven to 350°F. Grease the bottoms of three 8-inch cake pans. Place a round of parchment paper in each pan; grease and flour the bottom and sides of the pans.

2. In a large bowl, beat the butter and sugars with an electric mixer for 3 to 5 minutes or until light and fluffy. Beat in the eggs, one at a time, until well blended. Beat in the oil and the vanilla extract.

3. In a large bowl, combine the flour, baking powder, nutmeg, cinnamon, baking soda, and salt. Beat the flour mixture into the butter mixture, alternating with the eggnog, until the batter is well blended. Divide the batter among the prepared cake pans, smoothing the tops with a spatula.

4. Bake for 25 to 30 minutes or until a toothpick inserted in the center comes out clean. Cool the cakes in the pans on a wire rack for 10 minutes. Turn out from pans and cool completely.

5. Prepare the Cream Cheese Frosting according to the recipe on page 144. Stir in 1 teaspoon of rum extract. Spread a ¼-inch layer of frosting between the cake layers. Frost the top and sides with a thin layer of frosting. Refrigerate, uncovered, for 30 minutes until the frosting is firm. Frost the top and sides again with the remaining frosting. Sprinkle with additional ground nutmeg, if desired.

JAPANESE CHRISTMAS CAKE

✦ SERVES 6 ✦

Christmas cake is very popular in Japan on Christmas Eve, a holiday celebrated romantically in that nation. The three basic elements are sponge cake, whipped cream, and strawberries. This variation includes amaretto-marinated strawberries, which create a syrup that soaks deliciously into the soft, tender cake.

TOKYO
GODFATHERS
(2003)

While foraging for food in piles of trash on the streets of Tokyo on Christmas Eve, three homeless people discover a crying baby. The trio set themselves on a quest to return the abandoned baby to her parents, and the subsequent journey is one filled with adventure, self-discovery, and the spirit of generosity that the Christmas season brings out in all of us.

Cooking spray

2¼ cups cake or all-purpose flour, plus more for pans

1¼ cups plus 1 tablespoon granulated sugar, divided

2 teaspoons baking powder

¼ teaspoon fine sea salt

6 large eggs, yolks and whites separated and at room temperature

½ teaspoon cream of tartar

¾ cup whole milk

½ cup (8 tablespoons) unsalted butter, melted

1½ teaspoons vanilla extract

1 pint strawberries, sliced

1 tablespoon amaretto

Sweetened Whipped Cream Frosting (recipe follows)

Fresh mint, for garnish

1. Preheat the oven to 325°F. Grease the bottom of two 8-inch cake pans with the cooking spray. Place a round of parchment paper in the bottom; grease and flour the bottom and sides of the pans.

2. In a medium bowl, combine the flour, ¾ cup of the sugar, baking powder, and salt; set aside.

3. In a stand mixer, beat the egg whites with a whisk attachment on high speed until foamy. Add the cream of tartar and beat until soft peaks form. Add ½ cup of the remaining sugar and beat until stiff peaks form. Transfer to another bowl.

4. Add the egg yolks to the mixing bowl (you don't have to wash it first). Beat the yolks at high speed until they're thick and light. Gradually beat in the milk, melted butter, and vanilla. Beat the flour mixture into the yolk mixture.

5. Stir in about 1 cup of the beaten egg whites to the flour mixture to lighten the flour mixture. Gently fold in remaining egg-white mixture into the flour mixture. Spread evenly in the prepared cake pans.

Continued

6. Bake for 35 to 40 minutes or until a toothpick inserted in the center comes out clean and the top is golden. Cool in the pan for 5 minutes. Turn out onto wire racks and cool completely.

7. Combine the strawberries, amaretto, and remaining 1 tablespoon sugar in a bowl. Let stand for 30 minutes, stirring occasionally.

8. Place one cake layer on a plate and drizzle with a bit of the strawberry liquid. Spread with a layer of frosting, about ½ inch thick. Top with half of the marinated strawberries. Top with another cake layer and drizzle with the strawberry liquid, if desired. Frost the sides and top with the remaining frosting. Top with the remaining strawberries and garnish with mint.

SWEETENED WHIPPED CREAM FROSTING

→ MAKES ABOUT 5 CUPS ←

To keep whipped cream frosting from deflating or melting, it needs to be stabilized. Some recipes include gelatin, but this version uses very rich and flavorful mascarpone, which pairs nicely with the strawberry filling. Use softened cream cheese as a substitute.

1 (8-ounce) container mascarpone or cream cheese, softened

1 cup powdered sugar

2 cups heavy whipping cream, chilled

1 teaspoon vanilla extract

In a large mixing bowl, combine the cream cheese and sugar with an electric mixer. Beat until light and fluffy. Add the whipping cream and vanilla; beat until soft peaks form.

Bûche de Noël

➤ SERVES 10 TO 12 ➤

This traditional French Christmas cake is named for the giant yule log placed in fireplaces and burned through the twelve days of Christmas. The light whipped cream filling is delicate, so store in the refrigerator until thirty minutes before serving. Make ahead and freeze up to three months.

Cooking spray

⅔ cup all-purpose flour, plus more for pans

⅓ cup unsweetened cocoa powder

½ teaspoon fine sea salt

5 large eggs, yolks and whites separated, at room temperature

1 cup granulated sugar, divided

2 tablespoons unsalted butter, melted, or 2 tablespoons vegetable oil

1 teaspoon vanilla extract

¼ cup powdered sugar, plus more for dusting

Whipped Cream Filling (recipe follows)

Mocha–Cream Cheese Frosting (recipe follows)

For decorating: fresh cranberries, fresh rosemary, marzipan mushrooms

1. Preheat the oven to 350°F. Lightly grease a 15x10-inch jelly roll pan with the cooking spray and line with a sheet of parchment paper. Grease and flour the parchment paper.

2. In a small bowl, combine the flour, cocoa powder, and salt; set aside.

3. In a large mixing bowl, beat the egg whites at medium speed with an electric mixer until soft peaks form. Gradually whisk in ½ cup of the sugar. Transfer to a large bowl and set aside.

4. Add the egg yolks to the mixing bowl. Beat the yolks at high speed until the yolks are thick and light. Beat in the remaining ½ cup sugar, melted butter, and vanilla. Beat the flour mixture into the yolk mixture.

5. Spoon about 1 cup of the beaten egg whites into the chocolate mixture to lighten the chocolate mixture. Gently fold in remaining egg-white mixture into the chocolate mixture. Spread evenly in the prepared pan.

6. Bake for 15 minutes or until the cake springs back when touched on top.

7. Meanwhile, place a large, thin kitchen towel on a surface and sprinkle lightly and evenly with the powdered sugar. Immediately run a

Continued

8 WOMEN
(2002)

Another adults-only watch, this darkly comedic French musical is a mystery that rivals any Agatha Christie plot. Marcel has been murdered, and everyone is a suspect! This holiday whodunit features a cast of legendary French actresses who poke fun at all the over-the-top classic noir clichés. The unexpected twists come every few minutes, and you'll be kept guessing until the very end.

knife around the edges of the pan and invert it onto the prepared towel. Peel off the parchment paper. While cake is still warm, roll it up with the towel, starting at the long edge. Cool on a rack, seam side down.

8. Gently unroll the cake and remove the towel. Spread evenly with the Whipped Cream Filling and gently reroll. Cover and refrigerate for about 30 minutes. Spread the Mocha–Cream Cheese Frosting evenly over the cake roll. Cut a 3-inch diagonal slice from one end. Place the slice against the side of the cake roll to resemble a branch. Refrigerate until ready to serve and decorate as desired.

WHIPPED CREAM FILLING

MAKES 2½ CUPS

1¼ cups heavy whipping cream, chilled

¼ cup powdered sugar

½ teaspoon vanilla extract

In a large mixing bowl, beat the whipping cream with an electric mixer at medium high speed until very thick. Gradually whisk in the sugar, beating until soft peaks form. Gently fold in the vanilla.

MOCHA–CREAM CHEESE FROSTING

MAKES 2½ CUPS

2 teaspoons espresso powder

1 tablespoon water

1 (8-ounce) package cream cheese

½ cup (1 stick) unsalted butter, softened

2½ cups powdered sugar

⅓ cup cocoa powder

¼ teaspoon fine sea salt

1 teaspoon vanilla extract

1. In a small bowl, combine the espresso powder and water; set aside.

2. In a large bowl, beat the cream cheese and butter together with an electric mixer. In another bowl, stir together the powdered sugar, cocoa powder, and salt. Gradually add the cocoa mixture to the cream cheese mixture, beating at low speed until incorporated, then at high speed until smooth and fluffy. Beat in the vanilla and reserved espresso.

METRIC CHARTS

The recipes that appear in this cookbook use the standard US method for measuring liquid and dry or solid ingredients (teaspoons, tablespoons, and cups). The information on these pages is provided to help cooks outside the United States successfully use these recipes. All equivalents are approximate.

METRIC EQUIVALENTS FOR DIFFERENT TYPES OF INGREDIENTS

A standard cup measure of a dry or solid ingredient will vary in weight depending on the type of ingredient. A standard cup of liquid is the same volume for any type of liquid. Use the following chart when converting standard cup measures to grams (weight) or milliliters (volume).

STANDARD CUP	FINE POWDER (ex. flour)	GRAIN (ex. rice)	GRANULAR (ex. sugar)	LIQUID SOLIDS (ex. butter)	LIQUID (ex. milk)
1	140 g	150 g	190 g	200 g	240 ml
¾	105 g	113 g	143 g	150 g	180 ml
⅔	93 g	100 g	125 g	133 g	160 ml
½	70 g	75 g	95 g	100 g	120 ml
⅓	47 g	50 g	63 g	67 g	80 ml
¼	35 g	38 g	48 g	50 g	60 ml
⅛	18 g	19 g	24 g	25 g	30 ml

USEFUL EQUIVALENTS FOR DRY INGREDIENTS BY WEIGHT

(To convert ounces to grams, multiply the number of ounces by 30.)

OZ	LB	G
1 oz	1/16 lb	30 g
4 oz	¼ lb	120 g
8 oz	½ lb	240 g
12 oz	¾ lb	360 g
16 oz	1 lb	480 g

USEFUL EQUIVALENTS FOR LENGTH

(To convert inches to centimeters, multiply the number of inches by 2.5.)

IN	FT	YD	CM	M
1 in			2.5 cm	
6 in	½ ft		15 cm	
12 in	1 ft		30 cm	
36 in	3 ft	1 yd	90 cm	
40 in			100 cm	1 m

USEFUL EQUIVALENTS FOR LIQUID INGREDIENTS BY VOLUME

TSP	TBSP	CUPS	FL OZ	ML	L
¼ tsp				1 ml	
½ tsp				2 ml	
1 tsp				5 ml	
3 tsp	1 Tbsp		½ fl oz	15 ml	
	2 Tbsp	⅛ cup	1 fl oz	30 ml	
	4 Tbsp	¼ cup	2 fl oz	60 ml	
	5⅓ Tbsp	⅓ cup	3 fl oz	80 ml	
	8 Tbsp	½ cup	4 fl oz	120 ml	
	10⅔ Tbsp	⅔ cup	5 fl oz	160 ml	
	12 Tbsp	¾ cup	6 fl oz	180 ml	
	16 Tbsp	1 cup	8 fl oz	240 ml	
	1 pt	2 cups	16 fl oz	480 ml	
	1 qt	4 cups	32 fl oz	960 ml	
			33 fl oz	1000 ml	1 L

USEFUL EQUIVALENTS FOR COOKING/OVEN TEMPERATURES

	FAHRENHEIT	CELSIUS	GAS MARK
FREEZE WATER	32°F	0°C	
ROOM TEMPERATURE	68°F	20°C	
BOIL WATER	212°F	100°C	
	325°F	160°C	3
	350°F	180°C	4
	375°F	190°C	5
	400°F	200°C	6
	425°F	220°C	7
	450°F	230°C	8
BROIL		Grill	

INDEX

ABOUT THE AUTHOR

JULIA RUTLAND is a Washington, DC–area writer and recipe developer whose work appears regularly in publications and websites such as *Southern Living* magazine, *Coastal Living* magazine, and Weight Watchers books. She is the author of *Discover Dinnertime, The Campfire Foodie Cookbook, On a Stick, Blueberries, Squash, Apples, Tomatoes, Honey, Foil Pack Dinners,* and *101 Lasagnas & Other Layered Casseroles.* Julia lives in the DC wine country town of Hillsboro, Virginia, with her husband, two daughters, and many furry and feathered friends.